Faith is commitment to a conviction
for the best reasons available
aware that it may be wrong

Spirit is within us, drawing us on; spirit is around us, in mountains, oceans, and rivers, in music, art, and song, drawing us out. The whisper of spirit is heard by us, interpreted in different ways or plain drowned out. Given all we know of our universe, a creator God must be vastly big, "utterly other," transcendent. Given belief in Jesus Christ, God has been present among us and has laid down his life for his friends, "utterly us." Belief that the God of our universe should be lovingly committed to each one of us in the simple ordinariness of our lives is almost scandalous — or unbelievably wonderful (1 Cor 1:18-25 has both). The "utterly other" of a creator God is held together with the "utterly us" of Christ crucified. The whisper of spirit invites such faith. The phoenix church sustains such faith. There is a wonderful absurdity to Christian faith, weighed against the even greater absurdity of anything less.

The Whisper of Spirit

A Believable God Today

Antony F. Campbell, SJ

William B. Eerdmans Publishing Company

Grand Rapids, Michigan / Cambridge, U.K.

© 2008 Antony F. Campbell

Published 2008 by
Wm. B. Eerdmans Publishing Co.
2140 Oak Industrial Drive N.E., Grand Rapids, Michigan 49505 /
P.O. Box 163, Cambridge CB3 9PU U.K.

Printed in the United States of America

12 11 10 09 08   7 6 5 4 3 2 1

Library of Congress Cataloging-in-Publication Data

Campbell, Antony F.
The whisper of spirit: a believable God today / Antony F. Campbell.
p.   cm.
Includes bibliographical references.
ISBN 978-0-8028-4042-4 (pbk.: alk. paper)
1. God (Christianity). 2. Apologetics. 3. Faith.
I. Title.

BT103.C36 2008
230'.2 — dc22

2007043600

www.eerdmans.com

With gratitude to
CARRIE
without whom
this would not make
half the sense it does

Contents

CONTENTS

Contents

Acknowledgments

Much of the learning in this little book had its beginnings at what is now Claremont School of Theology and Claremont Graduate University, with particular gratitude to Rolf Knierim who showed me how to learn from the Scriptures. Much of the pastoral experience here is spread over more than thirty years in and out of Our Lady of the Assumption parish, Claremont, California. To Msgr. Bill Barry and Msgr. Tom Welbers and all at OLA, my deep thanks for wonderful hospitality and steady encouragement.

Many have helped in the shaping of this book; for a number of reasons, it would be invidious to name names. In a couple of instances, the normal acknowledgment of what I owe would be a grave understatement. I do want those who have been part of the book's making to know that I am deeply grateful. I also want readers to know that I have been greatly helped.

Introduction

As the tide turns and the full flow of life begins to move gently toward the receding ebb of age, I realize that I have always wanted my Christian faith to be justifiable as a respectable choice — probably better, an intelligent and reasonable choice. As a Roman Catholic, I have had a charmed life. In my early days in New Zealand, my family seldom went to the local parish church; my mother found other places for Sunday Mass. Family legend gave as reason that my eldest brother's imitation of the parish priest intoning the Gloria — glo-o-oria in excelsis Deo et in terra pax hominibus bolla wolla tartis (I think it was supposed to be "bonae voluntatis," peace to people of good will) — was too close to the bathroom singing of an overweight tenor lathering up under the shower. As imitation, it was much too accurate. I didn't go to a Catholic primary school or a Sunday school; much that I might have had to unlearn later I did not learn in the first place.

There were two pious Catholic women in the family: my mother and my godmother, who lived with us. As a youngster, I remember hearing fragments like, "Oh Nancy, have you heard what the silly little man has done now?" I didn't have to be particularly smart to know that the "little man" was probably the local bishop and that what he had done was certainly silly. It helped a lot for later serenity. Faith mattered and shaped your life; the details of local church politics did not matter all that much, and you shaped your life diplomatically around them. Those were the days when we got excommunicated for sending children to non-Catholic schools and were in trouble with the bishop if we went to

xi

a non-Catholic wedding. My father was a non-practicing Anglican; I would hear the two of them, mother and father, planning how to handle their social life and the weddings of their friends. Those were the days!

I joined the Jesuits with wonderfully mixed motives; pride was among them. To be a priest was to be sure of salvation; to be a Jesuit was to be sure of the best. Sweet God, what certainty, what arrogance! University studies took me into Hebrew, Greek, and archaeology. I learned to value the insight and wisdom of the ancients; I read about places with strange-sounding names, like Haçilar and Çatal Hüyük, neolithic towns existing in Turkey many thousand years ago. The thesis for my Masters was on the Palestinian Chalcolithic, around 3,250 BCE. Theology took me to France and the discovery that some of the Catholic Church's great theologians were, in the 1960s, still coming to terms with the experience of World War II (1939-45); they talked about Scripture and Tradition, but their theology was shaped by their experience from the war years. Then Scripture in Rome and Germany. Then California, parish life, and a doctorate. Finally, Australia and teaching in an ecumenical faculty. Being involved in the theological learning of people coming out of the Anglican, Methodist, Presbyterian, and Roman Catholic traditions, among others, imparts remarkable awareness of the richness and breadth of Christian faith.

"Intelligent and reasonable." Hans Küng has written that all great religions contain elements of belief, unbelief, and superstition. Acceptance of the reality of doubt is comforting, and highly respectable. Superstition permeates a lot more of life than most of us would like to admit, and it's not all that reasonable or respectable. Religious belief is often dismissed as old-fashioned and outmoded; often enough, up-to-date and supposedly sophisticated and informed circles hardly regard it as intelligent and reasonable. My specialty is Older Testament; my commitment is to a faith that is an intelligent and reasonable choice.

This is a book about faith; faith first, Christian faith later, and church after that. While I believe there is a clear logic to the book's structure, it is not always evident to readers. Spelling it out here will be helpful.

Introduction

Part One: Belief in God's Being

The book begins with the faith we all have: some believe in a world without a god; some believe in a world with a god. Either way, that is faith. My apologies to agnostics, but I fear complicating matters.

A second chapter touches on modern science (physics and cosmology). For many, modern science has replaced religious faith. It hasn't, of course. Modern science has replaced outmoded science.

Religion and science need not clash. Roger Penrose, emeritus physicist at Oxford University, writes:

> The purpose of this book is to convey to the reader some feeling for what is surely one of the most important and exciting voyages of discovery that humanity has embarked upon. This is the search for the underlying principles that govern the behaviour of our universe.[1]

The purpose of *The Whisper of Spirit* is to encourage in the reader a deepened awareness of what is surely one of the deepest, most spiritual, and ultimately most ecstatic journeys of humanity across the millennia. The goal of the journey: fuller awareness of and feeling for our restlessness in search of the rest that is the source of the existence of the universe.

The universe must first exist (in whatever primal condition) before it can behave. Existence is other than behavior. Religion claims God (or: a god) as the source of this existence. For some four to five millennia, it has sought to appropriate this. Christian theology, of course, goes a step further when it integrates this appropriation with the revelation of God in Jesus Christ.

What interests me most is the basis that grounds faith in a world with God. First, for Christians, it is not the Bible. The Bible is immensely valuable; however, it is direct evidence *of* people's faith, but it is not necessarily direct evidence *for* faith in God. Second, not the Chris-

---

1. Roger Penrose, *The Road to Reality: A Complete Guide to the Laws of the Universe* (New York: Alfred A. Knopf, 2005), p. xv.

tian church. It is too easy to point to where it has been wrong, too human, or whatever. I suggest one basis for faith in a world with God is the whisper of spirit that many of us experience. This whisper, sensed in our experience of ourselves and our world, can lead us to faith in a world with God.

Part Two: Faith in God's Love

But, what sort of a God? The whisper of spirit leads only to a transcendent God, a God who is "utterly other." For Christians, above all, belief in Jesus Christ as God's initiative in our midst leads to faith in a God who cares about us human beings. That belief can take several forms; it can give a depth and joy to human life.

Part Three: Faith and a Future Church

Finally, there is the question of how we support and nourish this Christian faith in a God who cares about us, who loves us. That leads to questions about the shape of a future Church, the phoenix church.

That is what this book is about. It is a careful and systematic unfolding of secure grounds for faith in the God who is "utterly other" and an equally careful and systematic reflection on the Christian faith in a loving God as an option for wisdom in today's world.

I believe it is important to situate theist and atheist on the same plane of belief. Otherwise, the "level field" is unfairly tilted. I believe it is important to recognize the place of modern science in our understanding of our world today. Beyond that, I believe we can hear the whisper of spirit. Atheist or theist, we both hear it; we react to it in different ways. Theists are led by the experience to an awareness of themselves that yearns for the ground of their being. The same experience leads atheists, I believe, to a sense of sheer wonder. The whisper takes theists to a God who is "utterly other"; it takes them no further. So a second, smaller part of the book turns to faith in Jesus Christ and the exploration, in Christian faith, of what it means that the God who is the ground of religious believers' beings should be concerned for humankind. The final part of the book looks to the institutional structures that might support and nourish such faith. Nothing wrong with institutions; where two or three are gathered, we've got an institution.

The contents page reflects this structure. Part One: belief in God's being — where our own experience of ourselves and our world can take us. Part Two: belief in God's love — where the Newer Testament and faith in Jesus Christ can take Christians. Part Three: what people in the future, grouped as church, can do to support and nourish such faith.

I use the term "faith" very broadly to refer to what is not demonstrable. It is what I choose as intellectually or emotionally acceptable, but not what I know by way of demonstration. Some people speak of faith as gift; I prefer the language of choice. As a committed theist, I choose faith in a world with God; that is how I interpret my experience. As I understand it, committed atheists choose faith in a world without God; that is how they interpret their experience. Nobody gives it to them; they do not believe there is anybody there to give it. The epigraph of this book claims that faith is commitment to a conviction for the best reasons available, aware that it may be wrong. "Commitment to a conviction": not a system of propositions, a way of life, or anything like that. "For the best reasons available": not superstition or anything like that. "Aware that it may be wrong": not knowledge that is demonstrable, or anything like that. Faith has been called "the assurance of things hoped for, the conviction of things not seen" (Heb 11:1). I hope the author of Hebrews would go along with my understanding, allowing me to insist that we do not short-circuit things by appealing to "pie in the sky when you die." We are entitled to hope that what we do not know for certain is true all the same; what we do not see can indeed be the object of our conviction.

This book is about the Who? Why? What? questions, the sort of questions most of us don't like to ask ourselves too often, if at all (e.g., Alec Leamas in *The Spy Who Came in from the Cold:* "And I don't like conversations about Life").[2] "Who am I? Why are we here? What meaning is there?" If we raised these questions too often with others, we

---

2. John Le Carré, *The Spy Who Came in from the Cold* (London: Gollancz, 1963), p. 42.

might well rank with the more intolerable of bores. All the same, they are questions that almost all of us raise with ourselves at some stage of our lives. Sometimes we come back to them. Most of the time, we live our lives in the routine of the ordinary — days, weeks, years. In the background, there are the answers we've given to our questioning or, as the case may be, the absence of answers. Once in a while, we pause and take stock, before life goes on again; or while life is going on we touch the depths and take stock. It is for such stock-taking that this book is written. Some folk, even cast away on a desert island, would not dream of it. As one friend said: "Tony, I was born in Boston, Irish and Catholic, and I've voted Democrat all my life. Of course there's a God." Then he added, almost as an afterthought: "Maybe there isn't." After that, the conversation got into deeper waters. But the lesson remains: If you don't want to take stock, don't — until you want to.

Good novelists have a feeling for human depths. Saul Bellow claimed that "each person yearns to have answers to abiding questions."[3] The yearnings may be stifled; the questions abide.

A Dutch friend says: "I ignore what I don't believe." It's one way of functioning, but it can leave gaping holes in the fabric of personal faith.

It will help to situate this book to some degree within its time and culture. Gilbert Murray (1866-1957), one of Oxford's great classical scholars, wrote of the shift from the time of the writers of classical Athens to those after the classical period, from an atmosphere in which the aim of the good citizen was to live justly, to help society, and enjoy the esteem of others to an atmosphere where "by means of a burning faith, contempt for the world and its standards, by ecstasy, suffering, and martyrdom," the good citizen hoped to be granted pardon for "unspeakable unworthiness," "immeasurable sins."[4] In the present time, I believe we have returned to something like Murray's first period, with concern for the good citizen to live justly, to help society, and enjoy the esteem of others; I trust we have turned away from "contempt for the world and its standards . . . [our] unspeakable unworthiness . . . immea-

3. Ruth Miller, *Saul Bellow: A Biography of the Imagination* (New York: St. Martin's Press, 1991), p. 28.

4. Jaroslav Pelikan, ed., *The World Treasury of Modern Religious Thought* (Boston: Little, Brown, 1990), p. 46.

surable sins." Without question, human beings are utterly other than God; that does not prevent God's love for them reaching out across the chasm of that otherness. This is the context within which this book is written.

Religious belief and scientific knowledge have often been seen in apparent opposition, rather on a parallel with superstition and sophistication, leaving people entrammeled (religion) or enlightened (science). As it has become clearer that both religion and science are seeking to articulate something of the mystery of the universe in which we live, they have often moved toward complementarity rather than opposition. As the basic attitudes in which both are grounded are better understood, the differences of territory are more easily accepted. For myself, I do not expect the mysteries of cosmology — especially in the light of relativity and quantum mechanics, string theory and branes — to be resolved by religion. But I do not expect to find the meaning of life in the mysteries of modern science.

Language requires precision. Language like "the scientific view" is loose and unfortunate. "Science" does not view the universe as causeless and accidental (see below); some scientists do. Beyond that, some scientists who say, for example, that there is no soul are speaking loosely and unfortunately. What they are entitled to say is that science has not found a soul, has not found evidence of a soul. In their own field, scientists do not yet have experimental proof of the existence of a number of things, for example, of the existence of a Higgs ocean (non-zero Higgs field). Theory requires them; experiment has not yet found them. Religious faith gets into trouble when it overstates its claims; so do scientists.

One further aspect of context needs to be spelled out. I do not accept what has often been taken for granted in the past, that religion is essentially bound to ethical behavior. I could wax lyrical on the preservation of power and maintenance of the status quo lurking beneath some apparently simple verities and religious truths. For me, religion is a matter of relationship to God, no more and no less. Naturally, a right relationship with God leads to right behavior; the relationship, of course, is primary. A right relationship with those we love leads to right behavior too; we know that. We also know that a lapse in behavior can be forgiven; it need not end a relationship. Should it be any different with God?

The great anti-religion thinkers of at least the nineteenth century were against some of the unjust and highly prejudicial social and cultural assumptions of the times in which they lived. Thank God, few of these social and cultural assumptions have lasted, and the power and privilege of churches no longer lean on them. It may be time to take a fresh look at ourselves. Such a fresh look has to look at religious faith in its entirety; restriction to Christianity or a given Western church would be absurd. At the same time, as a Roman Catholic my criticisms will be situated within my own church. Others are unlikely to have difficulty making the equivalent assessments for their own churches or faith communities. I believe that it is important for any faith to be deeply lived before one moves to criticism.

This book is about some of the most basic issues for Christians: faith, Bible, and church. It is based on a breadth of professional and pastoral experience; it demands genuine interest in the concerns addressed and a readiness for focused reading and seriousness of thought that are relatively rare. At the same time, it is not an academic book. There are minimal footnotes and few references to other studies; the book is too short and too wide-ranging for that. Much that is deliberately not included here (mainly European background) may be found in Hans Küng's *Does God Exist?*[5] The aim of this book is to lay out in simple, uncluttered form some of the basic and wise convictions that underlie a life of religious faith for Western Christians today and implications for the unfolding of that life as church in the future.

In many ways, this is a book of theory and theology. As long as we are aware that no one in their right mind would want to stay confined to the abstract realm of theological thought without the certainty of being freed for the deep living of God-filled life, we can read it freely — as I can write it freely. Evelyn Waugh, with a novelist's insight, has what is perhaps another way of putting this: "to know and love one other human being is the root of all wisdom."[6]

The factors that have people believing in a world with God are

5. Hans Küng, *Does God Exist?* (Garden City, NY: Doubleday, 1980).
6. Evelyn Waugh, *Brideshead Revisited: The Sacred and Profane Memories of Captain Charles Ryder* (Boston: Little, Brown, 1945), p. 45.

surely as many as the sands by the sea; the facets of that belief are as many again. This book does not offer anything like a full exploration of them. It provides the underpinning for them. In the Newer Testament, it is evident that Jesus took the reality of God for granted. Plenty of people are ready to take Jesus' word for it. Others may agree but also want to build on their own experience; after all, our perception of the world and the universe has changed enormously in a couple of thousand years. This book explores something of that building on our own experience.

We have learned so much in the last few hundred years and have been freed of so much ignorance and fear. Is our learning, above all our scientific learning, advanced enough now for us to be able to look more freely at aspects of experience that have always been there and are there still?

Readers will understand that this is not a book built on the gospel of Jesus Christ. I take that gospel for granted in my life. To recapitulate: this book has three parts. First, belief in a world with God. Are there grounds for such belief? If so, what are they? For many, belief in Jesus Christ leads them directly to their belief in a world with God. The first part of this book does not deny that route but takes a different one, exploring the whispers we experience that may lead us to a God who is "utterly other." The second part turns to Jesus Christ, not to learn about the God of Jesus but to explore the implications of a God who is committed to us. This approach does not deny what Jesus said of God; it does not depend on it either. This approach simply takes a different route with a different concern — which, by the way, explains why Part Two is relatively short. Finally, in the third part of the book, we explore how faith in God as "utterly other" and God as benevolently committed to us can be supported and nourished. The Christian church has taken many forms in the two thousand or so years of its existence — for example, in the East and in the West, before the Reformation and after it, etc. The phoenix church of the future (I belong in the post-Reformation West) may take forms that build on and extend beyond our present experience.

PART ONE

BELIEF IN GOD'S BEING

CHAPTER 1

Atheists, Theists, and Agnostics

There are at least three different ways in which people today view the world: seeing our world without a god; seeing our world with a god; seeing our world and believing they do not know enough to commit themselves about a god. The traditional terms are atheists, theists, and agnostics. One usage that is common among us is unfair and harmfully inaccurate; it speaks of believers and unbelievers. It is unfair because it destroys the level playing field of life, appearing to require a positive action of some (believers) while disclaiming it of others (unbelievers). It is inaccurate because all three groups are believers. Atheists see our world and believe there is no god; theists see our world and believe there is a god; agnostics see our world and believe the evidence on either side is not good enough to decide about a god. All are believers. If atheists could prove beyond doubt that there was no god, agnostics and theists would be up that fabled creek in a barbed wire canoe without a paddle. If theists had a cast-iron case for certainty, atheists and agnostics would be in similar trouble. No one, no human being, escapes the necessity of belief, of living in the uncertainty of faith rather than the hard-and-fast certainty of knowledge.

Central to our human condition is that all of us live in faith about the one aspect of human life that is of overwhelming importance to us: Is our being here due to God or is it unexplained? As the theologian Joseph Ratzinger put it emphatically, long before he became Pope Benedict XVI: "Every man must adopt some kind of attitude to the basic questions, and no man can do this in any other way but that of entertaining belief. There is a realm which allows no other answer but that of entertaining a belief, and no man can completely avoid this realm. Every man is bound to have some kind of 'belief.'"[1]

One day theoretical physics and the science of cosmology will, we hope, explain everything from after time zero; time zero itself — however it is described — is simply there, to be reckoned with.

Atheism: Belief in a World without God

Unless dogged by misfortune, atheists believing in a world without God can live full and worthwhile lives. Life-giving values can be endorsed without involving God. Very often, the culture we live in may present us with values of the highest order. Very often, those who for whatever reason do not believe in the existence of a god can choose to live their lives in the light of these values. Such lives can be of enormous worth.

Historically, "existence" has proved a difficult term in relation to God. God "exists" and we "exist," but the meaning of "exist" is radically different in the two cases. God is utterly other than us and God's existence is utterly other than ours. "Nothing" and "non-existence" do not help; in ordinary language they mean something different. As a student for priesthood, I was introduced to Thomistic notions of analogy and the three stages involved in any analogical affirmation. First, negative: purify the idea from whatever might be limited or not good. Second, positive: affirm whatever is good in the idea. Finally, eminent: exalt the idea to a level appropriate to God. Of course, this last step takes the idea beyond the reach of ordinary language, which is not hugely helpful. But then ordinary language is not all that helpful for God.

Those who believe in a world without a god can be intimate and committed partners; they can be wonderful parents to their children. There is no reason why they should not be, any more or less than any others among us. They can be protective of others, committed to justice in the family, the workplace, the nation, and the world. They can be committed to the highest ideals, whether in the arts or in the art of hu-

1. Joseph Ratzinger, *Introduction to Christianity* (London: Search, 1969), p. 41.

man living. It would be a fearful mistake to think that belief in a world without God inevitably condemned such believers to lesser levels of life and lesser values than those endorsed by believers in God.

Our ideals, whether we believe in God or not, are often not matched by our attainments. Jealousy, resentment, greed, manipulation, fraud — and all sorts of other evil — have their place in the lives of people across the human spectrum, irrespective of their ultimate beliefs. Beyond the satisfaction of absolute needs, there are relative needs met by competitive consumption, aimed at lifting us above and making us feel superior to others (cf. John Maynard Keynes).[2] Many of us appear to be wounded enough to fuel our sense of self-worth with transitory matters such as financial assets, social esteem, personal power, and the like. Such shortsightedness is not restricted to atheists.

Reflection will help readers refrain from thinking that evil is always done from base and evil motives. The human capacity for distorted vision is amazing. I think of a conversation between a bank robber and a priest-friend of mine. The man said: "You know, Father, you don't get more than about three thousand bucks in the average bank heist today. I need about ten thousand dollars to give my kids a decent Christmas. I've done a couple of successful jobs recently, but I'll need to do a third to make enough for Christmas." My friend was staggered and said: "But what about the trauma of some poor bank teller staring into the barrel of a gun? The terror could affect them for life." The reply was simple enough: "Yeah, I know, Father. I really regret that, you know, but I need the money if I'm going to give my kids a decent Christmas." It is a badly one-sided distortion of family values to assume that money automatically creates "a decent Christmas," but it is a good example of good values (family Christmas) being used as motivation for serious evil. Self-deception is common to us all; at its worst, it wreaks havoc — from the top of the corporate ladder to the bottom of the social pile. The Savings and Loan debacle and the Enron collapse could be singled out as examples in the USA; others abound at all levels around the world.

With that little clarifier out of the way, we can come back to those

---

2. John Kenneth Galbraith, *The Affluent Society* (Boston: Houghton Mifflin, 1958), ch. 10.

who believe in a world without God and look honestly at some of the reasons for such belief. It has been said that the root causes of atheism come down to two: the evil in the world (natural calamities and human viciousness) and the evil in the churches (ambition, power, prestige, wealth). This may be an oversimplification, but it is not a bad base for beginning to take stock.

The reality of suffering in the world is obvious enough. Some of it is the result of human freedom, the beastliness of human beings to each other, from across the street to across the world. Some of it is the result of the forces of nature, earthquakes, hurricanes, volcanoes, epidemics, and more. Many ask how a loving God can allow such suffering. "Allow" is loading the issue. Is the prevention of such suffering within God's power? The suffering is an obvious fact of human experience. God's relationship to this suffering — "How can a loving God allow such suffering?" — is a matter of theology. Does God allow it? Can God prevent it? Is God its source? These are theological questions, and their answers are neither obvious nor simple. In fact, we may not have adequate answers at all.

Certainly, believers in a loving God have no compelling answer beyond the strength of their faith in a loving God and their grief over the suffering; according to their faith, God too both loves and grieves. It is hardly surprising that those who do not share the strength of this faith should turn away from belief in such a God. Suffering and evil they see; God they do not see. Hearing those who believe in the power of God and confronted by the reality of suffering and evil, their conclusion is understandable; there cannot be a loving God.

Amartya Sen, Nobel-prize-winning economist, describing himself as "a non-religious person," comments: "Certainly the appalling world in which we live does not — at least on the surface — look like one in which an all-powerful benevolence is having its way. It is hard to understand how a compassionate world order can include so many people afflicted by acute misery, persistent hunger and deprived and desperate lives, and why millions of innocent children have to die each year from lack of food or medical attention or social care."[3]

3. Amartya Sen, *Development As Freedom* (New York: Anchor, 2000), p. 282.

Along with Amartya Sen, I have long had my doubts about "an all-powerful benevolence . . . having its way" in our world. I have faith in a God who is benevolent; I have no problem believing that the God who is "utterly other" is all-powerful. But, for whatever reason we cannot fathom, my experience does not encounter a benevolence "all-powerful" in our life and our world. Power, yes; physical power, no. Powerful, yes; all-powerful, no. Powerful in terms of invitation, encouragement, support, commitment, and challenge — yes. All-powerful in terms of the physical power of coercion (to prevent human evil) or causation (to prevent natural disaster) — no. Not in my experience.

The realization of the God who is the source of existence as "utterly other" can be theologically liberating. Some say: it is a weird idea that this God should love us. One can agree that it sounds weird, but with a God who is "utterly other," it is possible. Some say: nothing happens without God's willing it. From experience, one may not think so, but with a God who is "utterly other," who knows? Some say: God knows everything in the future. Reflection may lead to reluctance to claim this, but with a God who is "utterly other," who knows? And so on.

At the same time, "utterly other" applied to the God of spirit's whisper has to be used with care. The "other" is important to us; the maturing of our lives is reflected in the evolving relationship between ourselves and "the other" in an ever-widening understanding. "Utterly other" could be understood in an alienating sense as utterly apart from, estranged, and without commonality of any kind. Between Creator and creation there is a commonality, tenuous but real. The biblical image of humankind made in God's image and likeness catches something of this commonality (cf. Gen 1:26). The affirmation of the utter otherness of the God reached by human experience and the whisper of spirit is not the affirmation of incommunicability and the denial of any possibility of relationship. It is the affirmation of God as utterly big, utterly extraordinary, utterly beyond the scope of human language and ideas — transcendent. The theme is worth at least a chapter; all we can give it here is this paragraph. The vastness of the universe correlates with the vastness of God; that has to be enough for us here.

The experience of my life in so many ways is in complete agreement with Sen about all that is "appalling" in our world. Sen goes on: "I can

7

appreciate the force of the claim that people themselves must have responsibility for the development and change of the world in which they live. One does not have to be either devout or nondevout to accept this basic connection."[4] That is surely true, but I would not want to develop it as an argument supposedly to justify the benevolence of an all-powerful God who leaves us to work our own way out of our mess. As the chapters to come will show, my belief is that there is a benevolent God. My experience is that the "appalling" exists — in individual lives, in our world at large. I hold these together because I experience both. I experience the whispers that lead me to faith in God (and, through faith in Jesus Christ, to a loving God). I experience the suffering. It is part of why I am grateful for God as "utterly other." I do not understand. I am not happy with theories that seek to promote understanding here; for me, they sell too much short. I live with two sets of experiences. I trust that God — who as the Creator of our universe must in my eyes be all-powerful (powerful beyond understanding) — reconciles both benevolent power and human pain. It is part of why I am grateful for God as "utterly other." I believe in God's "benevolence" within human life; I do not experience God's benevolence as "all-powerful" within human life. The "utterly other" of God allows me to cope with that.

A long-lived strand of human religious tradition has believed that right living is rewarded and wickedness punished. If it didn't always seem that way, nevertheless it was believed that that's the way it was. In the Bible, many of the Psalms and Proverbs tended that way. The book of Job took the opposite tack, but at first sight not in a hugely helpful way.

The flat opposition may mirror the myopia that comes from theoretical wishful thinking at a distance from the reality of life, embodying a clear categorization of righteous and unrighteous, contrasted with the rather fuzzy clarity that comes from personal involvement with individual people. Reflections from Ratzinger hint in some such direction. He writes that if one takes the Sermon on the Mount seriously:

> The beautiful black and white into which one is accustomed to divide men changes into the grey of a universal twilight. It be-

4. Sen, *Development As Freedom*, p. 282.

comes clear that with men there is no such thing as black and white, and that in spite of all the possible gradations, which do in fact span a wide range, nevertheless all men stand somewhere in the twilight. To change the imagery, one could say that if the moral differences between men can be found to be total in the "macroscopic" realm, a microscopic, "micromoral" inspection discloses a different picture, in which the distinctions begin to look questionable.[5]

Perhaps Psalms and Proverbs tend in the direction of a piously unreal "macroscopic" realm and Job offers something closer to a "micromoral" inspection.

In the book of Job, two apparently unconnected questions are asked. The first question is given the satan (having the definite article — in Hebrew it cannot be a proper name here; "accuser" or "adversary" catches the meaning). Following the opening "Have you seen my servant Job? Good man isn't he?" from God, the satan puts the question: "Does Job fear God for nothing?" (1:9). Less formally: "Does all right out of it, doesn't he? Take away the good life and he'll curse you." In the story — and please, God, only in the story — God gives in and lets the satan loose on Job, as long as Job himself is spared. The result: a win for God; Job does not curse God. Questioned a second time, the satan argues that it would be different if he could have a go at Job himself. Appallingly, God allows him to. This time too God wins; there is no curse from Job. "Shall we receive the good at the hand of God, and not receive the bad?" (Job 2:10; cf. Job 1:1–2:10).

At first sight, story or not, God comes out of it very badly and Job seems rigidly stuck in a rut — praising God at any price. The core of the book is about much more.

The initial scenes are couched in folkloric terms; the dialogue located in heaven and the stereotyped agony on earth. Nevertheless, the question addresses a perennial human issue: the motivation behind religious faith. Can a religious believer worship God unselfishly or does self-interest inevitably get in the way? As the satan would say: they do

---

5. Ratzinger, *Introduction to Christianity*, p. 195.

well out of it, don't they? The answer in the book is positive; unselfish worship of God is possible. The story, however, leaves Job in a frighteningly painful situation, battered by the satan. The misery of Job's situation opens the way to the rest of the book.

The second question is put on Job's lips: "Why is light given to one in misery, and life to the bitter in soul?" (3:20). Some blind avenues may be closed off by the book of Job and a more fruitful direction hinted at, but no clear-cut answer is given. Job has three friends who show up to be with him in his misery. For seven days, they sit with him in silence; we have to admire them. Unfortunately, they then give voice to some basic human convictions. The author of Job puts some of the common human views on display where we are forced to look at them. "None of us is perfect, Job; no wonder you're suffering." "Hang in there, Job; it will be all right in the end. In the meantime, put your trust in God." Ironic, when we think that in the story it was God who gave the satan-figure a free hand. "The wicked always get their come-uppance; that's the way it is, Job. If you're not wicked, you'll be okay in the end." "Don't blame God for it." Anyway, "you deserved much worse." The discussion starts on a relatively friendly level; as it goes on, it gets a lot uglier and more hostile. Job, of course, gives as good as he gets. The upshot of it all: faced with suffering, we humans do not do too well.

Readers generally admire Job, as a character in the story, for sticking to his claim of personal innocence and integrity. He is portrayed insisting that he wants to confront God and have things out in legal argument. But at the end of the book, in the speech given God, humans and their fate, including Job's, don't feature at all. God talks about the origins of creation, the problems of meteorology, and the necessary care for the animal kingdom (Job 38–41). Human beings don't rate a mention. For all his courage and integrity in the earlier part of the poetry, Job appears to buckle. "I lay my hand on my mouth" (40:4); "I have uttered what I did not understand" (42:3).

Typical of the book, Job's buckling is highly ambiguous and uncertain. Christopher Booker, in a massive and insightful study of narrative covering the range of Western storytelling from its origins to today, speaks of Job's "abject capitulation" and Job's being "utterly crushed"; for Booker, Job ends up "accepting the power's [i.e., God's] rightful claim to rule over the world and himself [i.e., Job]."[6] Far from clear, despite being traditional, this view is at least highly ambiguous and uncertain; quite possibly, it is thoroughly wrong.

First, the strongest argument against Job's abject capitulation after being utterly crushed is found in the next three verses (42:7-9), undeniably tied to the poetry. The biblical text has the LORD say to Eliphaz the Temanite: "My wrath is kindled against you and against your two friends; for you have not spoken of me what is right, as my servant Job has" (42:7). If Job has spoken rightly of God, he can hardly have been utterly crushed and have buckled in abject capitulation.

Second, Job speaks of having seen God: "now my eye sees you" (42:5). This is puzzling, because *nowhere* in the book has Job seen God. God *speaks* to Job out of the whirlwind (38:1); God does not appear to Job as he so easily might have done. Throughout the book, Job has been hearing of God "by the hearing of the ear" (42:5); nowhere in the book has it been said that Job's eye saw God. Reference to the ear and the eye cautions against too facile a spiritualizing of this hearing and seeing. Possibly, listening to God speaking of God's creation of our earth and God's relationship to some of its animals has led Job to see God in a new light. At the limit, it is possible but unlikely that the voice from the whirlwind is "the living evidence of his [God's] presence," reflecting Job's "long search to find God" (e.g., 23:3, 9).[7] It would make eminent sense for God to be seen in this way and would help enormously in the understanding of the book; it would have been so easy to do so clearly and, alas, clear evidence is not there in the text.

Third, the last line given to Job in the Hebrew text (42:6) cannot be translated along the lines of "therefore I despise/abhor myself, and repent in dust and ashes" (NRSV/Booker). The issue has been recognized since the time of Moses Maimonides (1135-1204). The text does *not* say what tradition and translations have interfered to make it say. It is absurd to suggest that the basic direction of a biblical book of massive theological thought should be reversed in one final verse that is both

---

6. Christopher Booker, *The Seven Basic Plots: Why We Tell Stories* (London: Continuum, 2004), pp. 496-97.

7. Norman Habel, *The Book of Job: A Commentary*, OTL (London: SCM, 1985), p. 582.

uncertain and obscure. "The ambiguity is caused by the absence of an object for the verb. The meaning of the verse depends on the object supplied."[8] Tradition and translations that insert "myself," making the verb reflexive, do so from their own conviction and not from the biblical text. It is difficult to portray Job in the guise of "abject capitulation," as being "utterly crushed."

Finally, Job's first reply to God, who expects a response, is scarcely one of self-contempt and abject capitulation. With unwonted humility or perhaps subtle refusal, Job claims that he has said his bit and he will shut up. "I lay my hand on my mouth. I have spoken once, and I will not answer" (40:4-5). This is hardly self-contempt and capitulation.

The meaning of Job's last line (42:6) is probably best expressed along the lines of "I've had enough of all this palaver on the ashheap." Job has not given up his commitment to his own innocence, affirmed at the start of the book by both the narrator and God ("blameless and upright," Job 1:1, 8; 2:3). He may have given up the idea of settling the issue of suffering through legal debate with God (see, for example, 31:35-37).

In the previous verse (42:5), what does the narrative mean when it has Job say to God, "now my eye sees you"? A metaphorical seeing has been suggested: God is seen differently by Job after God's speech about the vastness of the world and its content. Alternatively, almost in despair, readers may step outside the book and suggest that Job forgets about legal argument and logic and simply sees the God he has encountered all these years. Both are possible suggestions. They are better than violating the known laws of Hebrew grammar and syntax. They are better than using a single obscure verse (42:6) to turn a whole book upside down for the sake of tradition. They may be good suggestions, but they are not answers to the problem of evil and the reality of suffering. They are not good enough to prevent people from believing in a world without God.

Where does one's eye see God? The Older Testament's Flood story may offer a glimmer of insight. At the beginning of the Flood narrative, it is said of God that "the LORD saw that the wickedness of humankind was great.... And the LORD was sorry ... and it grieved him to his heart" (Gen

---

8. Habel, *The Book of Job*, p. 576.

6:5-6). And yet, with no change at the end and "the human heart [still] evil from youth," the text has the LORD hang in with us (Gen 8:21-22). Can empathy and insight allow an all-holy God to remain in relationship with a less-than-perfect humankind or worse? (Note: not imperfect individuals in an otherwise estimable race, but ordinary individuals and a "less-than-perfect" race in a "less-than-perfect" world.) Can the eye of a Job figure see a grieving God? I have encountered the unutterably brutalized who in turn have brutalized unutterably and who, incredibly, have been found lovable. For me, the experience has been extremely rare but also unquestionably real. It holds massive sorrow and grief. It may be a pointer, no more, to how one can imagine the possibility of a grieving God, a pointer to how one's eye can *see* a grieving God. Grief for the unutterably brutalized; horror at the unutterable brutalizing; love for the lovable. Someone who has been utterly hateful in our sight may, with compassion, time, and steadily deepening knowledge, be found lovable. Dare we predict God's behavior?

Personal experience is one thing; integrating it into a personal theology is another. Pity help us if we let the two get far apart. It is complex and, with a God who is "utterly other," it is far from simple. There are multiple "times" to be aware of. There is horror at the unutterable brutalizing (done to "us" and by "us" to you), grief for the unutterably brutalized ("us" and you), and — at a later time and in changed circumstances — awareness of the lovable and the experience of loving. If there are multiple "times," there are multiple "standpoints." Among them: the power of compassion, the knowledge of deepening insight. There are extremes of feeling: brutality that is most hateful; love that is most treasured. All of this somehow holds together. It is complex. It may be beyond belief; unbelievably, it is not beyond experience.

The book of Job's narrative has God dismiss the theology of the friends. They have not spoken rightly of God. The narrative denies three standard human convictions: that suffering is deserved; that it will probably come right in the end for the innocent; that the wicked will be overwhelmed. Such traditions do not rightly reflect God: too bad for much of Psalms and Proverbs; too bad for much of human tradition. The narrative points in a possibly more fruitful direction: the experience of the relationship with God, independently of the baloney

13

mouthed by inadequate theology. It may be the best that God-believing thinkers can come up with. Can our eyes be opened to see a grieving God? It is complex. It may not fully satisfy. Nothing, no matter how satisfactory, takes away the suffering.

None of this reconciles those overwhelmed by the extent of appalling human suffering with the views of those who endorse a loving God (above all, those who blithely proclaim the goodness of Jesus, "meek and mild"). For many, the suffering and evil around us are powerful reasons for dismissing the idea of God as no more than a potent human delusion.

Before we come to the evil in the Church, it might be good to pause a moment on the simple power of human delusion. Most people are not evil, just weak or wounded. Superstition is a factor in secular human life; those who shun the 13th (day, hotel floor, etc.) may be atheists, theists, or agnostics. Superstition in matters religious is a different kettle of fish, and it would be good to be able to do without it. For many, religious belief is apparently a crutch to help them through life. Many others would prefer to be atheists rather than lean on such a crutch; one can hardly blame them. In many people's eyes, Jesus' claim "I came that they may have life, and have it abundantly" (John 10:10) is in flat contradiction with the lifeless living of too many churchgoing folk. The scandal is enough to make atheists of many of us. Christian faith should generate abundant life. In some regions, the apparent lifelessness of some who claim the name Christian, compounded by the appearance of weakness and fear, is enough to put many off any thought of a Christian God or Christian faith. For all the truth of this, space has to be found in our hearts for compassion. There are many ways of living life, and the more energetic of us can well do with patience and compassion for those not so energetic. It may be the fault of how faith is understood; it may be the weakness of the people understanding it.

In the final count, the issue of belief is not determined by the attitudes of others. In the final count, the issue of belief comes down to the reality of the experience of each of us. It is not the existentialist's exclamation, "If only Christians had risen faces." It is whether, for each of us, belief in a world with God would give us "risen faces" and abundant life.

The evil in the Christian church is fair reason to keep many at a distance from Christian faith. In recent times, that evil has worn a particularly evident and shameful face, that of sexual abuse, the tragic consequences of the non-observance of appropriate boundaries and professional standards. There is no question that such abuse is appalling and abhorrent. Prescinding from the church, its horror has been widespread in society for centuries. Its uncovering is likely to change social patterns substantially. The long-term implications cannot be fully foreseen. The transformations will almost certainly be broad and deep and are most unlikely to be restricted to the churches and similar bodies.

However, when I speak here of "the evil in the Christian church" as a reason to keep many at a distance from Christian faith, I have something else in mind. What I would call the primary evil in the Christian church is an evil done by some clergy to themselves: the insidious selling of their souls to the system in the quest for advancement, or the selling of their principles in the quest for power, pleasure, or superior living. Beyond that, if we look back over the history of the churches in almost any country, there has been a constant struggle for clerical power over people, a constant struggle for hierarchical power and class structures within the clergy. Kings and popes vied for power, princes and prince archbishops vied for power, merchants and monasteries were powers in the land.

Jesus Christ was an itinerant preacher, at the head of an unruly bunch of Galilean fishermen. Matthew has Jesus say, talking about John the Baptist, "Those who wear soft robes are in royal palaces" (Matt 11:8). The same Matthew has Jesus say of himself, "Foxes have holes, and birds of the air have nests; but the Son of Man has nowhere to lay his head" (Matt 8:20). All too many of the upper ranks among Jesus' followers have worn splendidly soft robes and lived in palaces that might have been the envy of many a king. Good reasons abound; scandal abounds as much. Great cathedrals were raised around Europe to the glory of God and the sublimity of the human soul; they were also intended to be bigger and better than the one in the neighboring town. It was important that the spiritual (often represented by the church) should not bow to the injustice of the law (often represented by the State). Often, though, it seemed more important in the conflict that the churchman should not bow to the statesman. The areas of ambiguity and unclarity will always be there. The witness of saints will be there. Nevertheless, it would require massive dishonesty and willful ignorance not to confess the sinful ambition, greed, and lust of too many representatives of the churches that claimed to speak for Christ. Unfortunately, the blame is not the exclusive prerogative of those at the top of the tree. Lower down and on a lesser scale, the luxuries of living can outweigh the values of the spirit.

The old conundrum returns. It is not the folly or the weakness of others that can ground our decisions about ourselves. The decision for belief in a world with God or belief in a world without God is made by each of us for ourselves. The scandal of others may erode the value of their witness to the faith they proclaim; it need not disqualify the value of that faith.

Whatever the reasons that lead to belief in a world without God, they need not impact negatively on the quality of human living. One consequence however is that there is no Creator to appeal to for the past and no future with God to be looked for in the hereafter. What happens at the end of life for those who believe in a world without God is much the same as was believed, in the Older Testament, to happen for Abraham, Isaac, and Jacob. They believed in God; to the best of our knowledge, they did not believe in anything that we might call an afterlife. The possibility of life continuing in some form after death plays a minimal role in the canonical Hebrew Scriptures. In the Older Testament of the Orthodox and Roman Catholic churches, for example, belief in an afterlife is expressed in the deutero-canonical books; in the Older Testament of the reformation churches, such books are not reckoned as canonical Scripture and are termed Apocrypha. Atheists do not normally look to life after death; neither did the bulk of the Older Testament. The value of life and its focus are to be found in the here and now; it is fruitless to look behind or beyond.

This means, of course, that those who believe in a world without God face a further decision, beyond that choice of faith. Will they live for themselves alone, or will they live for themselves within the larger community they touch? The selfish choice to live for me and mine is understandable; after all, few others will remember us for long when we are gone. On the other hand, the community of the human race is there and my life can have greater richness of meaning if it enhances human-kind. It is a choice that each must make.

Theism: Belief in a World with God

Unless dogged by misfortune, theists believing in a world with God can live full and worthwhile lives. The reasons for their belief we can look at later. Here our concern is rather with the way theists live. It is enough to say for now that, at deepest base, their belief in God is probably grounded in a whisper of the spirit, to be discerned within them when they are at their stillest. Along with that is likely to be a sense of wonder, the wonder that anything is at all, a sense of wonderment that they themselves and all the elements in the world around them give evidence of not being self-sufficient, not being adequate to account for their own existence. The ultimate ground of wonder: Why am I here? Why are we here? Why is there something rather than nothing? Other grounds for wonder: the oceans, the mountains, the stars. We are born, we live, we die; the galaxies are born, live, and die; "all is in flux" (Heraclitus). For most, there is more to it than that, but as far as ultimate ground goes these are good places to begin. What matters most is the recognition that belief in God is not a funny internal feeling or a sense of weakness or dependence; it is based on a perception of the reality of what is.

Belief in a world with God can take many forms. If our text here were to encompass them all, it would be unbearably turgid. So I had better admit that I have little time for the God of the fundamentalists and fear-mongers. To my mind, a God of the bean-counters would be largely wasting divine time. The choices we must make about a loving God will occupy us later. Later too, we will explore the credibility of belief not just in God but in a loving God. For now, we will take it as deferred.

Most of those who believe in a world with God live in the wholeness of a universe complete in thought and meaning — and seldom dwell on it. Without a God, a universe doesn't have a soul to call its own. There is not a reason for its existence; it just is. Many an atheist might claim that God is just a smart word for an absence of good reason. Perhaps it is not; perhaps God is a smart word for a reality that cannot be named any other way. Physicists can tell us the most marvelous things about the beginnings of our universe or multiverse. What no physicist should claim to tell us is whether what was — almost infinitely hot and almost infinitely dense and so on — was created or uncreated. The laws of physics do not make that claim. Those who believe in a world with God do make that claim, not on the basis of the laws of physics but on the observation of themselves as harboring the "whisper of spirit" within them, not holding within them or within all that they can observe adequate reason for their existence.

"The preeminent mystery is why anything exists at all."[9] The word "God" covers the massive mystery of our origins. The whisper of spirit within us is witness to the existence of such a mystery. The whisper from the sense of wonder — before the inadequacy of all that we can observe to account for itself — obliges us to turn to what we cannot observe. To opt for belief in this "massive mystery" we call God is to claim wholeness and completeness for our universe, to take away from it and from our lives the taint of being a fluke, a mere happenstance of chance in the infinity of space and time. Of course, we can always ask the smart-aleck question: "Who caused God?" The answer is eminently simple: "uncaused" is part of the definition, part of the massive mystery; it comes with the belief. If someone doesn't like it, they don't have to believe in it; but then they needn't bother those whose beliefs differ from theirs — and, of course, shouldn't be bothered by them.

For those who believe in a world with God there is a constant companionship. It is not a usual companionship. It is not the caring love of a partner that may sustain one during absence, but is reaffirmed by presence. It is not the companionship of friends that is sustained and recharged by meetings. It is an elusive presence, often unnoticed, based only on belief, but, like so many faith-filled commitments, available when needed, when adverted to.

The youngster, asked by his teasing uncle what he'd learned in religion class that day, said he'd learned that God was everywhere. "Oh, so

9. Martin Rees, *Our Cosmic Habitat* (Princeton, NJ: Princeton University Press, 2001), p. xi.

God goes to the races, does he?" said uncle, trying to sound shocked. "Oh no," said his nephew, "God doesn't go to the races." "But I thought you said he was everywhere," said uncle. "That's right," he said. "That's why he doesn't go to the races. He's there already." So simplistic, so naïve, and yet so right. And if God is everywhere, then wherever we are and whatever we are doing God companions us. Those who believe in a world with God have this belief available to them. They may be too busy to enjoy it, but it's there. Like the prayer of the British naval officer in the charge of a frigate aground in the Yangtze River and under pressure from the Communists: "Oh God, if in the busyness of this day, I forget you, do not you forget me." (I am told that this prayer goes back to the time of those fighting Cromwell; it has ancient and valued lineage.)

Accompaniment in life leads on to companionship beyond it. Those who believe in a world with God are entitled to belief in companionship with God after life in this world. What such life might be like we have absolutely no idea; we believe it will be with God and with others — and that is enough. "What we will be has not yet been revealed" (1 John 3:2). An aspect of this gives enormous weight and worth to human living. It is the aspect of permanence. What we own and what we have achieved externally remain behind when we die. Only what we are — and what others are because of us — may last beyond the grave, ours or theirs. For those who believe in a world with God and life with God, their beings need not be snuffed out at the end of human life.

Whatever good is done accrues to the growth of the person; whatever is less than good diminishes the person. Death may end the process; it may not end the person. Whatever has become remains as what now is. For some this is not a pleasant thought: "No way. In heaven, we will be perfect!" I am not so sure. If, with God, we are to be perfect, I do not see how the seriousness of this life is maintained. This life has to be serious; there is too much about it that is not funny. It makes little sense to believe in a life with God that does not include acceptance of God's love. To know that we are loved even when we know we are imperfect is not an unhappy state. In my experience, there can hardly be greater happiness than when we know our weaknesses are known — impatience, insecurity, resentment, whatever — and we are loved. Should it be otherwise with God?

19

If we have come from nowhere and are going nowhere, from nothingness into nothingness, whatever we have done we leave behind us; whatever we are, we cannot take with us, for we have no place to go. For those who believe in a world without God, goodness in this life is motivated by the conviction that, as a rule, worth and joy in life grow out of goodness. Those who believe in a world with God can add to that motivation both the permanence of who they are and also the goodness that becomes part of them or the evil that diminishes them. Who they become is who they may be permanently. The reality of this permanence is something those who believe in a world with God can all too easily forget on a day-to-day basis. Who we become now is who we will be. It is a great incentive to ensuring that who we are is in line with who we want to be. Daydreams are all very well; reality is the permanence of what is, who we become. The incentive to right living is enormous. To some people, the idea is unpleasant, even outrageous. It may, however, be right.

If one is a believer in an unconditionally loving God (or, if you prefer, an unshakably benevolent God) — the reasonableness of this belief will be discussed below — there is a further quality to daily living. It is one thing to be companioned in life; it is an even greater thing to be loved. To know oneself loved from moment to moment and day to day is a source of greatest completeness and joy. It is also a matter of faith; we believe we know we are loved. Most of us know enough of the complexities of human motivation to recognize the place for flaws in such faith. Lovers on earth have vastly more sensory proofs of their love than we can ever have with God. To balance this, there can be a faith in God's fidelity, constancy, and understanding. It can be rock solid; for many, rock solid but with all the fragility of belief.

All of this needs further discussion below. For now, it will have to be enough to say that it need not be wish-fulfillment nonsense or weak-minded delusion.

Honesty, however, requires that we look at the areas of fear and venality, scruple and superstition. These have dogged religious behavior for centuries and cannot be ignored. Fear and venality go hand in hand. If faith in God was accepted in terms of an all-seeing judge and a celestial accountant, such fear is understandable. If human authorities encouraged such fear and profited from it, we are entitled to speak of venality. The power of the churches has often supported structures that were venal; the power of the churches has often benefited from the fear of people. It may take a while for such sin to be widely recognized, but recognized it is. A social culture that aided and abetted such fear and venality is not surprising; it is most regrettable. Scruple and superstition thrive on such fear and play into the hands of the venal. They come, above all, from needs that are all too human and unlikely to vanish from the scene.

According to some, God can be dismissed as "pie in the sky" (leaning on Marx) or "big daddy in the sky" (leaning on Freud). True enough, if belief in God is used to encourage submission to oppression instead of resistance; true enough, if belief in God becomes a crutch for infantile helplessness in the face of life. If belief in God, as Creator of our human universe and lover of our human lives, demands justice, opposes oppression, and supports confidence and courage, then such belief in God reveals the shortsightedness of these caricatures of religious faith. Like taxes, weaknesses and crutches may be always with us; like taxes, they can be regarded as simply part and parcel of human living.

In this context, God is not "Mr. Fixit" — committed and loving, yes; but no, not "Mr. Fixit." That God should be believed to be more powerful than we are is not surprising. That God is seen as not being humanity's filler of gaps should not be surprising. Deeply committed and loving friends can be sources of support, encouragement, and challenge; they do not do for us what we cannot do for ourselves. Christian portrayals of David and Goliath have all too often pictured the defenseless little fellow up against the fearsome giant. Only God could miraculously save David and Israel. Why well-informed people let themselves swallow such misguided nonsense may point to some Freudian need for "big daddy" to take care of us. David was King Saul's armor-bearer. In societies where the king led his forces into battle, the armor-bearer to the king was not a little fellow. David swapped gear with Jonathan, Saul's son and heir; Jonathan was hardly the runt of the royal litter. David's sling — a military weapon for killing, not a schoolboy's slingshot for playing — was in those days the ideal long-range weapon to take out the veteran infantryman. What role did David's faith in God play? As so often in Davidic stories, it prevented him from being paralyzed by fear and enabled him to do what he had the ability to do — overthrow the oppressor. God was far from a Mr. Fixit; faith may have steadied David's nerve.

To those who believe in a world with God, their faith can be a source of support, challenge, and invitation, to all that they see finest in the potentialities of human living. Faith in a loving God cannot tolerate injustice or inhumanity. If such believers accept that God loves them, they need to accept that God also loves others — painful as that may sometimes be. Observing the human capacity for unchecked injustice and inhumanity, they take into their belief the grief and sorrow of God. They take into their lives a commitment to eliminate injustice and inhumanity — at least, as far as they are able.

A faith in God that supports and invites such living is a pearl to be treasured.

Agnosticism: Belief That Only "Undecided" Is Appropriate

I must admit to having doubts about agnosticism; maybe I just do not know enough agnostics at sufficient depth or have not read enough about agnostic views. I can see the logic of arguing for three options: that there is no god; that there is a god; that we cannot know enough to make a decision appropriate. This side of the grave, it is logical. But beyond the grave, as far as we know the options reduce to two: either there is god or there is no god, either we continue or we cease. I find myself believing that agnostics, down deep, are probably committed to one or the other option but keep it a secret from themselves. Theoretical agnostics may be a rare species; practical agnostics may be legion — but that's another story.

It has been said of some religious leaders that they display remarkable flexibility, sitting on the fence with their ears to the ground. Remarkable, but not sustainable. In life, there are many situations where we have to make decisions without all the knowledge we might like to have; we have to choose jobs, partners, and so on. Do our insides really let some of us go through life without inner commitment on one of the biggest decisions we will ever face? Logic may say we simply do not know enough to commit to a yes or no on the question of a god. But there is more to life than logic. So I have my doubts about the inner reality of agnosticism. Can human insides remain equally balanced on an issue as important as whether or not there is a god and the goodness of that god? I know that mine can't. Like many, I live with doubts but, whether I like it or not, my insides have opted for the existence of God. So I am skeptical about agnosticism and I do not know enough agnostics to be convinced differently.

This may be unfair to agnostics, but it is where I am as I write. I have not come across anything that helps me make out a more acceptable or plausible case. To the question "Why are we here?", faith in a world with God offers an answer and faith in a world without God declines that answer. The agnostic resists an answer and declines faith.

In his *Life of Pi*, Yann Martel had relatively friendly words for atheists, but was not so well disposed toward agnostics.

> Atheists are my brothers and sisters of a different faith, and every word they speak speaks of faith. Like me, they go as far as the legs of reason will carry them — and then they leap. . . . I'll be honest about it. It is not atheists who get stuck in my craw, but agnostics. Doubt is useful for a while. . . . But we must move on. To choose doubt as a philosophy of life is akin to choosing immobility as a means of transportation.[10]

Right or wrong I do not know. The problem is there. Between the agnostic on the one hand and the theist or atheist on the other, space must be left for subtle matters of character, disposition, and style.

The passive or practical agnostic probably represents a much larger band of the population than the pollsters can get their figures on. The passive agnostics may be too busy getting on with the business of living to bother about the meaning of it all. To hit the depths of decision, we need to stop and stay stopped for a while. When, by disposition or cussedness, we do not stop, we may let a life go by in passive agnosticism. No loss but ours!

10. Yann Martel, *Life of Pi: A Novel* (Orlando, FL: Harcourt, 2001), p. 28.

CHAPTER 2

Contribution of Modern Science

The age-old questions are always with us: Why instead of nothing is there something? How come we are here? What does it mean? The questions will not go away; they cannot be dismissed as abstract because they concern us in the core of our being. Knowledge (i.e., factual and demonstrable), of its very nature, will not answer them; if there are to be answers, they have to come from faith (i.e., arguable, but nondemonstrable). Modern Western philosophy is indebted to Descartes and his "I think, therefore I am" (human existence). Universally, however, moderns may make the claim "I believe, therefore I am human" (human condition). When pondering the ultimate, all of us are reduced to belief; none of us can lay claim to factual knowledge in relation to the ultimate issues. Despite the evidence and all the reasons we rightly turn to, on the ultimate questions we humans are reduced to belief — all of us.

The contribution of modern science to the issue of faith is straightforward. (Modern physics and cosmology would be technically more accurate than the general "modern science"; I trust those affected will excuse the use of the more general term.) Once upon a time, not so very long ago — probably after Copernicus and Galileo, certainly after Newton — science was seen as a source of certainty and knowledge, replacing the world-picture that had flourished in the Middle Ages, in which the outward and inward worlds fitted together so perfectly. In its place, a new understanding emerged in which religion was seen as far from certain and lost in the insecurity of belief. In many areas where medi-

25

eval religious faith had provided answers, science showed these answers to be wrong and provided better ones, their certainty assured by experimental testing. At the level of ordinary living, there may still be truth in this perception; beyond the level of the ordinary, it is no longer the case. Science was once thought to have all the answers or to be capable of producing them. Now science has far bigger questions and has to live with the hope that one day theoretical answers may be forthcoming, with experimental testing perhaps possible. We can count on such answers being utterly unordinary.

The world is not the way we see it; we have got used to that. There are atoms and molecules we cannot see; smaller still, there are electrons, neutrons, and protons — even quarks and more. There are electromagnetic waves (like for radio and TV) that pass through solids (like us and the buildings we use). In the great blue yonder, above the smog, there are black holes and clumps of dark matter. Unquestionably, there is more to our world than our eyes can see. Notionally, we have got used to this. One of these days, we may have to get used to more.

A major contribution of modern science lies in providing a level playing field on which theists and atheists alike choose their faith, whether in a world with God or a world without God. No longer does science appear biased against religion; both confront an uncertain world and, from different viewpoints, wonder about its meaning. However, while the metaphor of the level playing field holds truth, it holds risk too. The "games" played on the field are quite different. Science deals with the measurable (matter, process); religion is involved with the immeasurable (spirit). We do not touch spirit; spirit touches us. Our senses cannot measure spirit; in its own way, spirit measures us. Science looks to the nature of matter; in the context of contrasting religion and science, religion seeks to find worthwhile meaning in life.

With the theories of general relativity and quantum mechanics, we have become more aware of the extremely large and the extremely small. Both, unfortunately, involve aspects beyond the boundaries of our current observational facilities. Quantum mechanics imposes a boundary in principle on certain aspects of observation. All of this brings into question the concept of science as "observationally refutable." At best, we may have to do without it for a while.[1]

Richard Dawkins asks the question "Are science and religion converging?" and answers with a plain, blunt "No."[2] Approached his way, of course, his answer is totally right, pillorying the claims that end up practically redefining science as religion. Approaching the question as we do here, Dawkins's answer is probably thoroughly wrong. Confronted with nature as Newton never was, science today is experiencing the complexity and uncertainty that religion has always had to live with. For those religious believers who deny such complexity and uncertainty, there is the timeless sigh: "Sancta simplicitas!" (translational equivalent: [the naïveté of] sainted simpletons).

To anticipate aspects that will be touched on below, one recent candidate for preeminence on the stage of the physical sciences, inflationary cosmology, is a remarkably good example of this interplay between religious faith and scientific hypothesis. Brian Greene's description leaves plenty of room for belief in either a creating God or, to the contrary, belief in a universe that owes its existence to happenstance: "in inflationary cosmology the bang happened only when conditions were right . . . and that need not have coincided with the 'creation' of the universe. For this reason, the inflationary bang is best thought of as *an* event that the preexisting universe experienced, but not necessarily as *the* event that created the universe."[3] Lee Smolin says much the same: when we have it, a quantum theory of gravity will have to answer "very mysterious questions about the origin of the universe, such as whether the big bang was the first moment of time or only a transition from a different world that existed previously";[4] later, "before that [the Bang] there may be nothing to see — or, at the very least, if there is something it will most likely look nothing like a world suspended in a static three-

---

1. Cf. Roger Penrose, *The Road to Reality: A Complete Guide to the Laws of the Universe* (New York: Knopf, 2005), p. 1020.

2. Richard Dawkins, *The Devil's Chaplain: Reflections on Hope, Lies, Science, and Love* (Boston: Houghton Mifflin, 2003), p. 146.

3. Brian Greene, *The Fabric of the Cosmos: Space, Time, and the Texture of Reality* (New York: Knopf, 2004), p. 286.

4. Lee Smolin, *Three Roads to Quantum Gravity* (New York: Basic Books, 2001), p. 5.

dimensional space."[5] Back then, there was massive contrast with the commonsense experience of our everyday life. In the early moments of the universe, inflationary cosmology postulates enormous density, unthinkable heat (technically, 10^{28} degrees — more than some thousand billion billion times the temperature at the core of the sun), infinitesimal brevity (the tiniest fraction of a second — technically, around 10^{-35} seconds), and unbelievable speeds that all absolutely defy the possibilities of our imaginations. "A violent growth spurt, ballooning from submicroscopic to astronomical size in the blink of an eye."[6] Says Greene: "This means that in a brief flicker of time, about a trillionth of a trillionth of a trillionth of a second ATB [after the Bang], the size of the universe increased by a greater percentage than it has in the 15 billion years since."[7] Plenty of room exists for plenty of belief — either way: with or without God.

Cyclic cosmology, another recent candidate for preeminence, while leaving plenty of room for belief in a world with or without God, is again an example of massive contrast with the commonsense experience of everyday life. According to one version of such cosmology, our three-dimensional world of everyday living exists within a "braneworld" we cannot see, one of at least a pair, perhaps more. Two of these braneworlds, one of them enveloping us, collide (irreverently: the Big Splat, taking the place of the Big Bang), spend more than a trillion years rebounding from the collision, and ultimately return to collide again.[8] All of this immensity is occurring outside our commonsense world and outside our awareness.

One day, perhaps, experiment will have sorted out with clarity and certainty the processes from the origin of the universe. What those processes cannot do, not now and not in the future, is determine how what was came to be. Whatever happened to whatever was, the question will always be there: Did God's activity play a role in giving existence to what

5. Smolin, *Quantum Gravity*, p. 65.

6. *The New York Times*, "Astronomers Find the Earliest Signs Yet of a Violent Baby Universe," nytimes.com. March 17, 2006.

7. Brian Greene, *The Elegant Universe: Superstrings, Hidden Dimensions, and the Quest for the Ultimate Theory* (New York: Norton, 1999 and 2003), p. 356.

8. Cf. Greene, *Fabric of the Cosmos*, pp. 404-10.

we encounter as "what was"? "Giving existence to" is simply the transition from "was not" to "was."

Physics apart, the questions we all face are basic: Who are we? How do we come to be here? What is our worth? Long, long, long ago, the psalmist wondered about it: "what are human beings that you are mindful of them, mortals that you care for them?" (Ps 8:4 [NRSV]). Eons before, people probably asked themselves that question; if there are eons to come, people will probably still be asking the same question. Right now, of course, each of us needs to ask it for ourselves.

After Albert Einstein, Max Planck, Niels Bohr, Erwin Schrödinger, Werner Heisenberg, and so many others, modern physics has opened up vistas for belief in God that are totally unexpected. Previous generations did not dream of them. In the past, we knew that God's world was utterly different from ours; God lived in eternity, unfettered by all that fetters us. Now, we know that our own world too, as sketched by modern physics, is utterly different from the everyday world in which we live. Much of what follows may be verified across the works in the Bibliographical Note. Specific references are given where appropriate.

It has been said that in 1900 Planck "launched the quantum revolution."[9] Einstein's theory of special relativity dates to 1905 and his general relativity to 1915. To single out a couple of other moments among many, Schrödinger formulated the equation initiating quantum mechanics in 1926, and Heisenberg did the same for the uncertainty principle the following year. Britain's Paul Dirac developed the quantum theory of the electron and the theory of antiparticles. America's Richard Feynman is credited with one of the next steps, associated with the term quantum electrodynamics. It goes on. We trust physicists to know what it is all about; theoretically, much is still in process. We can leave details to the specialists but the upshot is painfully clear. The intuitive image we have of the commonsense world we live in is accurate enough for the distances we deal with and the speeds we move at. But if we move to the macroscopic (immense distances and enormous speeds) or the microscopic (infinitesimally small distances and masses), our own world is totally different from our perception of it.

9. Penrose, *Road to Reality,* p. 502.

Does it sound weird? It should. The probabilistic nature of quantum theory worried Einstein, and yet it followed from some of his own insights around photons. Is modern physics missing a trick somewhere or is the human mind, with its memory of the past and no equivalent for the future, playing an outrageous trick on reality? We do not know. For the moment, modern physicists appear not to know for sure either. Perhaps in the generation of our grandchildren's grandchildren, they will know; perhaps they will have to wait a little longer. Meantime, we bear with the standard comment of the physicist: perhaps these theories are totally absurd in the light of our commonsense perceptions, but they are verified with astonishing accuracy in countless experiments. For now, it tells us one thing for which we can be grateful. Given that our world is vastly more complex than we can ever hope to imagine, is it the least bit surprising that God should escape the limits of our understanding? For centuries, theologians called it mystery. It still is mystery, but today it is just that little bit more okay for it to be mystery. After all, so much else is.

The move away from the "commonsense" perception of our world can be systematized around at least three moments of theoretical tension.[10]

1. The tension between Newton and Maxwell — where the laws of motion are in tension with the laws of electromagnetism. The tension was resolved by special relativity.
2. The tension between Newton and Einstein — where gravity is understood as an instant influence and where it is understood that no influence is faster than the speed of light. The tension was resolved by general relativity.
3. The tension between general relativity and quantum mechanics — fundamentally, between the macroscopic realm and the microscopic. The tension is recognized; by many, it is believed or hoped that string theory may offer the potential for a resolution, but it is far from being fully unfolded.

10. Cf. Greene, *Elegant Universe*, pp. 5-6.

One way of putting it would be that in the "middle kingdom," between the microscopic and the macroscopic, Newton's laws still hold firm; beyond that "middle kingdom" however, in the new empires of micro- and macro-, they hold no sway.

Cosmological theory in modern science fascinates me. Two aspects in particular hold me in thrall: first, the intricacy of the utterly small in our daily world; second, the speeds, distances, densities, and temperatures involved in our understanding of the universe, from its origins until today and into the future. Above all, our commonsense experience of our world is left intact while being coupled with a realization that what we see is not at all the way ultimate reality is.

Commonsense experience is fine for everyday speeds and distances. But things change when we talk about the extremes of the range, such as the speed of light, or huge interstellar distances and minute sub-atomic distances. We live in a world delineated by the twin realities of space and time; physicists are obliged to merge both into a single reality, "spacetime." We rely on the stability of time for the timetables of trains or planes, for making interstate or international phone calls, etc. In modern physics all time is relative, and at vast speeds and distances this matters. An observer in a distant galaxy who, when *at rest,* is contemporary with *our now,* when walking *away* from us can be contemporary with a time many years into *our past;* more than that, walking *toward* us, the same observer in the same galaxy can be contemporary with a time many years into *our future.* It is not a question of waiting for light to travel the enormous distance; it is a matter of sharing as contemporary — that is, present right now, this very instant — periods that are years apart by our experience of time.[11] Unbelievable? Of course — but experimentally confirmed. Einstein found it seriously worrying. Not surprising. But that's physics.

Some Examples

Two stages need to be acknowledged. First, general relativity and quantum mechanics have introduced us to the world of the extremely large

---

11. Cf. Greene, *Fabric of the Cosmos,* pp. 132-39.

and the extremely small and made us aware of a reality radically different from day-to-day experience. Most of this is observably tested and accepted as certain. We can describe it broadly as "confirmed and accepted." Second, these developments have led and will lead to the further unfolding of theory — in particular the minuteness of strings, the intangibility of multiple dimensions (small or large) and, more speculatively, the immensity of branes. This unfolding may not be open to observable testing and in some cases may remain at the level of untested and unverifiable beauty. For all that, we can describe it as "awaiting confirmation and acceptance."

Seen as Confirmed and Widely Accepted

First, most of us non-physicists when we think about the expanding universe imagine galaxies hurtling through space at ever-increasing speeds. Having accepted the theory of general relativity, physicists know better. If they are careful with their language, they speak of a space that is expanding and hurling the galaxies apart. Does it sound weird? It certainly does, but apparently that's the way it is. We may think of the void beyond earth's atmosphere as the realm of absolute nothing. For physicists it is filled with gravitational fields that hold planets in orbit and stars in place. There is no empty void between the galaxies either but the reality of expanding space. Extraordinary!

Second, many of us tend to think of the Big Bang (its equivalent was first suggested around 1930 by a Belgian astrophysicist and priest, Abbé Georges Lemaître) in images of some celestial form of creative fireworks. Physicists, when they think about it, knowing that the entirety of our universe has to have been squeezed smaller than a grain of sand, are aware of space at that moment as infinitesimally small, density as massively heavy, and temperature as unbelievably hot. Extraordinary!

Third, most of us, when we try to conceptualize our expanding universe, think of a steady rate of expansion out from the Big Bang to where we are now. The theory of an inflationary universe counts on an infinitesimally short burst of extraordinary expansive energy (for a tiny fraction of a second) shortly after the Bang, then a far longer period of decelerating expansion under the impact of gravitational attraction (seven billion years or so), and finally a period of accelerating expansion. The speeds postulated for receding galaxies in our expanding universe now are unbelievable enough. What is postulated for that fraction of a second of extraordinarily expansive energy is way beyond the range of belief. Extraordinary! How simple life was before modern science took over.

Awaiting Confirmation and Acceptance

We are used to operating comfortably in three-dimensional space with time as a fourth dimension. These days, string-theorists ("M-theorists") tell us there are in fact ten spatial dimensions around us, with time as the eleventh. Extraordinary! M-theory is a newcomer in modern physics; along with loop quantum gravity, it may prove to be the unifier of relativity and quantum mechanics. Our everyday world has three spatial dimensions (breadth, width, and height) and time — a total of four dimensions in all. M-theory requires an additional seven space dimensions. Six of these are curled up in tiny shapes (called Calabi-Yau shapes), to be found at every point in spacetime; the seventh is a bit of a free-radical. We are talking minuscule spaces, billions of times smaller than an atom. For all that, it stretches the boundaries of belief; but string theory demands it. Until something better comes along, we had better believe it. Quite probably, some combination of string theory and loop quantum gravity will provide the something better.[12] It is unlikely to give much support to common sense. Only time will tell.

Beyond the unbelievably small, modern cosmology deals with dimensions and origins that are huge. The Big Bang was a hugely long time ago, a little less than some fifteen billion years; the density of matter was almost impossibly huge, cramming the whole of our universe into less than a pinhead; the temperature correlative with the density was hugely high. Was there a "before the Bang"? We do not know; we can theorize about possibilities. Of course there was an "after the

12. See Smolin, *Quantum Gravity*, pp. 185-93.

Bang"; we are it. Its early course can be mapped out mathematically; it is totally out of the range of our experience.

If an inflationary cosmology theorizes a universe "so enormous that the region we are able to see even with the most powerful telescope possible, is but a tiny fraction of the whole universe,"[13] it would be totally out of the range of our experience. The mind boggles at the thought of just how big God would have to be allowed to be. Certainly "utterly other."

Some Mind-Boggling

Allowing God to be big enough to be thought of in matching terms with the vastness of our universe is challenge enough. The ancient psalmist pondered how the God responsible for the heavens should bother about us humans ("when I look at the moon and stars, what are we that you care for us?" Ps 8:3-4 [Heb., 8:4-5]). Today, we can ponder how God can conceivably be big enough to be responsible for the universe. Three examples will help bring home to us that all is not as we see it and that what is may be other than we imagine.

First, the "two-slit" experiment; it is justly famous in the history of quantum physics. It had its origins in the early nineteenth century when Thomas Young demonstrated that light moved in waves, despite Newton's view that it was composed of particles. When light was passed through two slits, an interference pattern resulted that could only come from wave motion (interference pattern: akin to ripples intersecting, with reinforcing and canceling occurring). But then quintessential particles, such as photons or electrons, faced with two slits and logically required as particles to go through one or the other, still generated interference patterns — even when released only one at a time.[14] Particles behaved like waves. That was clear and shocking, but more was to come. When experimentally observed, the particles behaved like particles (no interference pattern); when not observed they behaved like waves (inter-

---

13. Greene, *Fabric of the Cosmos*, p. 285.
14. Cf. Greene, *Elegant Universe*, pp. 97-103.

ference pattern). One way of expressing this, even more bizarrely, is to say that the particle goes through both slits simultaneously — in fact, follows all possible trajectories (Feynman's "sum-over-paths"). Since all this is fully confirmed by experiment, we end up being forced to accept, in Feynman's words, that nature is how nature is — absurd.[15]

As regards experimental observation, it was found that photons "knew in advance" whether observation was going to occur or not. Uncanny! It gets uncannier. Not only did particles sometimes behave like waves and waves sometimes like particles; in one particular experiment, photons were observed "acting as both wave and particle at the same time."[16] "Absurd" was Feynman's word earlier about nature, but confirmed by experiment; "too crazy to be true" is Lee Smolin's about something else, which survives all attempts to disprove it;[17] it is all certainly at odds with our day-to-day commonsense experience. If God escapes our commonsense experience, we should not be surprised.

The second example is often referred to as "Bell's theorem." In fact, it goes back to a thought experiment proposed in the early 1930s by Einstein himself, Boris Podolsky, and Nathan Rosen (therefore "EPR") to rebut aspects of quantum theory and the uncertainty principle. In the mid-1960s, John Bell, an Irishman working in Geneva, proposed an experimental approach that could prove EPR right or wrong; but it was technically impossible at the time. Culminating in the early 1980s with Alain Aspect and colleagues working in Paris, experimenters achieved the impossible: created the technology, did the experiments, and proved Einstein and company wrong. All of us would be on the side of Einstein and company — and, of course, be wrong.

The example involves two utterly mind-boggling quantum concepts that here we will keep to the barest minimum of detail. They are "superposition" and "entanglement."

Superposition is the recognition that an element which must be either A or B is *both* until observed. It is not an issue of the observer's not

15. Richard Feynman, *QED: The Strange Theory of Light and Matter* (Princeton, NJ: Princeton University Press, 1988), p. 10.

16. John Gribbin, *Schrödinger's Kittens and the Search for Reality* (Boston: Little, Brown, 1995), p. 120.

17. Smolin, *Quantum Gravity,* p. 178.

knowing whether the element is A or B; it is an issue of the element being *both* until it is observed. Formulations vary; for example, Brian Greene: "particles hover in quantum limbo, in a fuzzy, amorphous, probabilistic mixture of all possibilities."[18] Small wonder Einstein was troubled.

Entanglement is the situation where certain properties of two particles are related in such a way that when the appropriate question (e.g., A or B?) is decided for one particle, it is also decided for the other. The gist of Bell's theorem, experimentally verified by Aspect and others, is that the outcome is achieved *simultaneously* (i.e., instantaneously) for both particles, no matter the distance between them — a universe apart, for example. Simultaneously, instantaneously, no matter the distance apart. Totally bizarre! As Einstein insisted, it is not supposed to be that way; but it is.

Those sharing Einstein's concerns may be comforted to find their difficulties present among some of the best specialist minds. Roger Penrose names three approaches common among physicists: (a) idealists — quantum mechanics allows us to compute probabilities, but it does not provide us with a picture of "reality"; (b) realists — the unitarily evolving quantum state completely describes actual reality; (c) positivists — they have no truck with "wishy-washy" issues of ontology, claiming they have no concern with what is "real" and what is "not real."[19] As Stephen Hawking has put it: "I don't demand that a theory correspond to reality because I don't know what it is. Reality is not a quality you can test with litmus paper. All I'm concerned with is that the theory should predict the results of measurements. Quantum theory does this very successfully."[20]

Third and finally, in moments of concentration it can happen that we fail to notice how fast time passes or we forget where we are. We tend to blame ourselves — absentmindedness, dementia, or some such. In quantum physics, thanks to Heisenberg's uncertainty principle, there is no question of blame. Instead, in the microscopic realm as

---

18. Greene, *Fabric of the Cosmos*, p. 112.

19. Penrose, *Road to Reality*, pp. 782-85.

20. Stephen Hawking and Roger Penrose, *The Nature of Space and Time* (Princeton, NJ: Princeton University Press, 1996), p. 121.

a matter of principle, we can be precise about a particle's position or its velocity (technically: momentum), but not about both. And that's the way it is. The more precise we are about one, the less precise we can be about the other. Leaving free will aside, in a Newtonian system (therefore, above the sub-atomic world) if our knowledge were infinite (I am told "deterministic chaos" explores the details of this "infinite"), we could describe exactly how the universe would be from any point on. After Heisenberg (within the sub-atomic world), with infinite knowledge we may know what the infinite possibilities are; we would also know, with infinite certainty, that we cannot know which of these possibilities will eventuate. God might breathe a sigh of relief, except that God would probably not be the least bit surprised, having known this from all eternity. While no conflict between these need exist, the balance is symbolic.

Once upon a time (after Newton), science was respectable and faith was unbelievable, as it were. Now science is verging on the unbelievable and faith in a world with God is becoming a respectable option.

Drawing on Brian Greene (well aware that others concur), we can develop more extensively what was touched on earlier in this chapter.

> A common misconception is that the big bang provides a theory of cosmic origins. It doesn't. The big bang is a theory . . . that delineates cosmic evolution from a split second after whatever happened to bring the universe into existence, but *it says nothing at all about time zero itself. . . .* It [the theory] tells us nothing about what banged, why it banged, how it banged, or, frankly, whether it ever really banged at all.
>
> The term "big bang" is sometimes used to denote the event that happened at time-zero itself, bringing the universe into existence. But since . . . the equations of general relativity break down at time-zero, no one has any understanding of what this event actually was. This omission is what we've meant by saying that the big bang theory leaves out the bang. . . . This approach leaves unanswered the question of what happened at the initial moment of the universe's creation — if there actually was such a moment.

The inflationary bang is best thought of as *an* event that the preexisting universe experienced, but not necessarily as *the* event that created the universe.[21]

Greene's "if there actually was such a moment" allows for the possibility of an eternal universe. Theologians should not mind that; philosophy allows for it. Greene's view that "no one has any understanding of what this event actually was" leaves space for the possibility of divine creation. Theologians would not mind that either. There is room in plenty for an extraordinary God or an extraordinary fluke.

Reflections

Somewhere between our beginning and our now, our planet Earth took shape. At some time, life emerged and eventually humans were present. At what point a relationship to God was possible for our predecessors, I prefer to leave in the unknown of mystery. We do not know; there is little point in uncontrolled surmise. We talk of tools and abstract thought. The capacity for relationship belongs there somewhere; I doubt that we can pinpoint it with any semblance of accuracy. I am content to leave it to mystery and the unknown; in the present state of our knowledge, there is little else we can do. If we accept God's choice of an evolutionary path toward the fullness of creation, we may accept God's opting out of certain aspects of planning and control. The movement toward intelligent and relational life need not be linear; developments that end up not going anywhere are inevitable.

We can discuss this in terms of the various pathways that originally led to relational life. We would be unwise to assume that this issue of the capacity to achieve relational awareness applies only at the beginnings of the human race. In the light of periods of incredible inhumanity, the possibility has to be entertained of individuals who were never enabled to develop the capacity of relating to another. This too I prefer to leave in the unknown of mystery.

21. Greene, *Fabric of the Cosmos*, pp. 272, 519, n. 2, and p. 286.

What can be measured and calculated is more easily reckoned with. In modern theory, the entire universe we can observe is assumed to have been compressed into a total space considerably smaller than an atom — the sort of size that makes a pinhead look large. We cannot possibly imagine our entire universe — not just our galaxy, the Milky Way, but the entire universe with its billions of galaxies — compressed into less than a pinhead. But we can realize that, in such a case, being so incredibly compressed would make it very, very hot. Calculations suggest a temperature (Kelvin) just after the Big Bang of ten to the thirty-second power, that is 10 with 32 zeros after it. Most of us don't have the time to even dream of the multiplication involved. It will help to realize that this is literally billions of times hotter than the center of the sun. To sum up: hugely heavy, hugely hot, and hugely long ago.

Believers in Christian faith are monotheists; we believe in one God. Theologians realize that within the reality of one God they have to allow for what we might call two aspects in our knowledge of God. There is the aspect of God here among us, God whom we can dare to describe as "utterly us," Jesus Christ, who is son of God and son of Mary, who is Jesus-God. Christians believe that, in Palestine a couple of thousand years ago, Jesus lived pretty much as the rest of us do. Jesus is an aspect of God we can talk about and almost understand. The other aspect is the side of God that is "utterly other" — the God we cannot hope to understand, of whom we cannot properly speak and of whom we had therefore best be silent.[22] We may not like being sentenced to silence, but mystery can reduce us to near silence, leaving only the gasps of wonder and awe. The unity (oneness) of God is not at stake, it is taken for granted; what is at stake, as theologians know, is the capacity of human language and imagination, needing to be stretched. God is mystery. Modern science can help us in coming to terms with the limits of our ordinary perception of reality and our understanding of it. Small wonder that, at the top, scientists and religion people understand each other.

As we have noted, common sense is problematic for both science

---

22. Ludwig Wittgenstein, *Tractatus Logico-Philosophicus* (London: Routledge & Kegan Paul, 1961; German original, 1921; first English translation, 1922), p. 7: "Whereof one cannot speak thereof one must be silent."

and religion. The common sense that was in such perfect harmony with classical Newtonian physics is no longer in harmony with the modern physics of general relativity and quantum mechanics. Classical physics works well at the sizes and speeds we deal with in our commonsense lives. At the sizes and speeds of the macroscopic (very big) or microscopic (very small), classical physics does not work well at all. From the beginning, common sense has been problematic for religion. The greatest temptation troubling religious faith is the attempt to keep God down to commonsense size. For example, there is the absurd language used of heaven — as someone put it in German, "auf nassen Wolken sitzen und Hallelujah singen" (sitting on wet clouds singing Halleluiah); there is the caricatured image of God as an old man with a long white beard. Nowadays, common sense troubles both modern physics and religion. Maybe humanity is making progress.

Once upon a time, science and religion seemed to be at each other's throat, engaged in a life-and-death struggle. Both claimed more than was their right; both have come to recognize the boundaries of their respective territories. For religion, the primary concern is with the relationship between the uncreated and the created. For science, the primary concern is with the laws of the created. The great Bengali thinker, Rabindranath Tagore (1861-1941), described science as "mysticism in the realm of material knowledge."[23] In science and religion, two mysticisms meet.

I have used the language of "extraordinary God or extraordinary fluke." In a John Updike novel, "the scientific view of the universe" is characterized as "ultimately causeless and accidental."[24] "Causeless" balances a traditional description of God as the "uncaused cause." Two pairs emerge:

(1) Atheistic view of the universe: causeless
    Theistic view of the Creator God: uncaused cause
(2) Atheistic view of the world: accidental
    Theistic view of the world: desired

---

23. Rabindranath Tagore, *The World Treasury of Modern Religious Thought,* ed. Jaroslav Pelikan (Boston: Little, Brown, 1990), p. 149.

24. John Updike, *Toward the End of Time* (New York: Knopf, 1977), p. 34.

The first pair ("causeless") offers two options. For a believer in a world without God, what *we do see* (the universe) is accepted as causeless, uncaused; for a believer in a world with God, what *we do not see* (God) is accepted as causeless, uncaused. In the second pair ("accidental" or "desired") a huge act of belief is required in both cases. This can be said only of the beginning itself; after the beginning, in either case, the theoretical analysis of the unfolding process is the task of the physicist. That our universe is a cosmic accident is philosophically possible; but its origins may need to have been so fine-tuned and complex as to be almost unbelievable. That our universe is the desired product of a Creator God is equally almost unbelievable; equally, it is also possible. One might argue that more than *possible* it is *highly probable,* if theory postulates the need for the origins to be so extremely fine-tuned and complex.[25] Discussion of how either of these possibilities might have come about is fascinating but outside the scope of a book like this.

By way of summary, we can say that religion should be deeply grateful to modern science. Once upon a time (as we have noted), religion had to appeal to mystery, while it was felt that science spoke a language of limpid clarity. No more. Once, science worked from experimentally established facts, accounting for the world of experience; these facts often appeared to be in conflict with the claims of religion, especially historical claims. Now, modern physics brings home to us how little we understand of the world in which we live. In the world after Newton, science was clear, in harmony with the world of experience, and fully capable of explaining that world. The Bible was not in harmony with the world of experience and did not explain it. Since Newton's day, two things have changed: first, it has been recognized that the Bible has other functions than explaining things; second, modern physics is no longer in such harmony with the world of day-to-day experience. In many ways, Newtonian physics seemed to stand the Bible on its head; in many ways, general relativity and quantum mechanics have stood Newtonian physics on its head. The modern physicist is confronted with a

---

25. E.g., Martin Rees: "we owe our very existence to a difference in the ninth decimal place" (*Our Cosmic Habitat* [Princeton, NJ: Princeton University Press, 2001], p. 128; cf. pp. xvi-xvii).

world in stark contrast with everyday experience; the stark contrast is confirmed by experimental results. It is as if belief were as deeply involved in physics as in religion. Theologians and physicists understand more of each other as they struggle to understand more of our world. The Newtonian understanding of the material world left room for discovery, but little room for mystery. His world was "as we see it." Due to recent developments, uncertainty and mystery have entered science. The world, especially in its microscopic and macroscopic dimensions, is no longer "as we see it."

The great unanswered question is: Why believe that a God who is "utterly other" should care the least little bit for the — sheerly on a statistical basis — infinitesimal speck (what Carl Sagan describes as "a grain of sand in a cosmic ocean"[26]) that is our human race in all the vastness of the universe? The lifetime of our observable universe is reckoned in billions of years; the lifetime of our human race is vastly shorter. Why believe God cares?

Even understood as concerned, God's care can be envisaged across an almost infinite range, from deep love coupled with almost total distance (some loving families find themselves obliged to be that way; for example, parents with alienated children) to intimately shared responsibility for almost every detail of life (some lovers find themselves that way). The range embraces a multitude of imaginable possibilities.

The question remains unanswered: In view of the vastness of the universe, why believe that a God who is "utterly other" should care the least little bit for the physically trifling speck that is us and our world? Why in any imaginable possibility should we believe God cares for us in any way at all? Attending to that is the task of Part Two of this book.

In Physics, Where to from Here?

It is important to keep Brian Greene's avowal in mind: "If these ideas are right — and I should emphasize that they have yet to be rigorously proven even though theorists have amassed a great deal of supporting

26. Carl Sagan, *Broca's Brain* (New York: Random House, 1974).

evidence — they strongly challenge the primacy of space and time."[27] The challenge to physical science to understand our universe is there, the theories to do it are at hand, the rigorous proving is yet to be done.

Reflection at the end of a long book leads Oxford's Roger Penrose to the recognition of "deeply mysterious issues about which we have very little comprehension." To move forward in such areas, "we shall need powerful ideas, which will take us in directions significantly different from those currently being pursued."[28]

A certain point of agreement can be found amid the competing theories. Roger Penrose: "Mathematical coherence is far from a sufficient criterion for telling us whether we are likely to be 'on the right track' . . ."[29] Brian Greene: "Until our theories make contact with observable, testable phenomena, they remain in limbo — they remain promising collections of ideas that may or may not have relevance for the real world."[30] With echoes of Scylla and Charybdis, Paul Halpern says of Swedish physicist Oskar Klein, "he saw himself as a mariner steering a course between the two deadly extremes of stodgy practicality [experimental facts] and whimsical imagination [theoretical speculation]."[31] The theories are at hand; the rigorous proving is yet to be done. The theories are at hand (Brian Greene favors string theory; Lee Smolin, of course, loop quantum gravity, with significant input from string theory and a few others; Stephen Hawking and Roger Penrose, in their different directions, something else). The rigorous proving is yet to be done. An avowed optimist, Smolin believes the experimental tests will be invented. Most optimistic of all, he believes this final outcome is not far away.[32]

Given a bit of lightheartedness and some serious oversimplification, we can say that the two British heavyweights, Stephen Hawking (Cambridge, "no boundary") and Roger Penrose (Oxford, "twistor the-

27. Greene, *Fabric of the Cosmos*, p. 485.

28. Penrose, *Road to Reality*, p. 1045; for background, see Steve Fuller, *Kuhn vs. Popper: The Struggle for the Soul of Science* (New York: Columbia University Press, 2004).

29. Penrose, *Road to Reality*, p. 1014.

30. Greene, *Fabric of the Cosmos*, p. 493.

31. Paul Halpern, *The Great Beyond: Higher Dimensions, Parallel Universes, and the Extraordinary Search for a Theory of Everything* (Hoboken, NJ: Wiley, 2004), p. 114.

32. Smolin, *Quantum Gravity*, pp. 210-11.

ory") disagree with each other and neither agrees with string theory; elsewhere (mainly the USA), the devotees of string theory and loop quantum gravity disagree with each other and everybody else. Agreement is about as far away as the parousia; for layfolk, a tad puzzling. Nowadays, science and religion have more in common than either would ever like to admit.

"Observable, testable phenomena" may be within our reach; it is also possible that they are in principle beyond our reach. Stephen Hawking, commenting on the hopes for a more powerful particle accelerator (the Large Hadron Collider), remarks: "We may be able to determine whether or not we live on a brane."[33] "We may be able to" implies the possibility that, alas, we may not be able to. The utterly small may, in principle, be beyond the reach of observation. In fact, in principle, observable horizons and quantum limits may in many cases preclude observable testing.

What is theoretically thinkable, thanks to the beauty of mathematics, may not always be experimentally testable, due to the inadequacy of current equipment or the cost of equipment capable of such observational testing — or due to matters of principle such as quantum uncertainty or smallness below the Planck scale (therefore undetectable). The outcome: we may have to live with the possibility that what can be elaborated mathematically may not be verifiable by physical testing. We may have to live with uncertainty.

A comment by Roger Penrose may presage a shift in our understanding of science: "The well-known philosopher of science Karl Popper provided a reasonable-looking criterion for the scientific admissibility of a proposed theory, namely that it be *observationally refutable.* But I fear that this is too stringent a criterion, and definitely too idealistic a view of science in this modern world of 'big science.'"[34]

Current theory in physics and cosmology struggles with strings and loops (associated predominantly with the very small) and branes (associated predominantly with the very large). In due course, theory may unify these or go beyond them or recognize that deciding between them

---

33. Stephen Hawking, *The Universe in a Nutshell* (New York: Bantam, 2001), p. 200.
34. Penrose, *Road to Reality*, p. 1020.

is excluded in principle. For now, we do not know. It is possible that we will never know (in terms of experimental confirmation). It is possible that, at best, we may come to believe (in terms of theoretical agreement). Religious believers may be stunned or, worse, incredulous. They should not be surprised. Accepting the possible inevitability of belief, physics may leave us in much the same space that religion does — but concerning quite different realities.

A grand unifying theory, if it emerges, may make life theoretically simpler for the physicists; for the rest of us, it is likely to make life practically much more mysterious. We will still experience ourselves living in three dimensions of space; the arrow of time will still be experienced as flowing from past to future. Experimentally proven or no, the reality surrounding us may be invisibly mysterious.

Religionists would be most unwise to gloat; too many of them are far from comfortable with the uncertainty of faith. Finding that belief has its place in both science and religion may help bring both into non-competitive balance, but their concerns are not the same. Religion is concerned with the Creator; science is concerned with the created. Religion is about relationship with the one who is believed to bring into being; science relates to what has become, what already is in being.

Bibliographical Note

For the interested reader's ease of access, two comprehensive treatments have been drawn on and can be recommended: Brian Greene's *The Elegant Universe* and *The Fabric of the Cosmos;* the issues are, of course, far more widely discussed. In my close reading of a dozen or so participants in the discussion, I have found some to be marvelous and some conceptually impenetrable. I would recommend as a good complement to Brian Greene's balanced studies, the Hawking-Penrose debate (*The Nature of Space and Time,* but with equations galore) and Roger Penrose's comprehensive work (*The Road to Reality,* also with abundant equations); to add further balance, there are Lee Smolin's *Three Roads to Quantum Gravity* and Paul Halpern's *The Great Beyond.* An extensive literature exists to keep us informed; Greene's *Elegant Uni-*

verse lists some thirty-five titles for further reading (pp. 427-28), and his *Fabric of the Cosmos* lists more than sixty (pp. 543-44), with limited duplication. A most enjoyable and remarkably comprehensive popular account of the origins of much that is now accepted science is given in Bill Bryson's *A Short History of Nearly Everything.* Particularly enlightening is its emphasis on the erratic and unsteady advance of scientific knowledge from discovery to awareness and, above all, to acceptance. This book went to Eerdmans in April 2006. Later that year, a new book by Paul Davies appeared, *The Goldilocks Enigma: Why Is the Universe Just Right for Life?* (Allen Lane, 2006); the U.S. equivalent is *Cosmic Jackpot: Why Our Universe Is Just Right for Life* (Houghton Mifflin, 2007). It belongs here.

CHAPTER 3

Contribution of Bible and Church

The ultimate decision about ourselves, whether we are committed to belief in a world without God or a world with God, is far too important to be left to the superficial. Recent sociology suggests that people join specific churches under the influence of friends or acquaintances.[1] Deeper than that is the question why people think they should be in churches at all. Faith in a world with God has to be founded on more than social convention, wish fulfillment, laziness of mind, whatever — or it isn't founded on much at all. Naturally, faith — theist or other — comes to a lot of people initially from their family and surroundings. Our interest here is the later adult appropriation of that faith or movement to that faith. The stages of human and faith development have been explored in specialist depth (for example: Erikson, Kohlberg, Fowler, Kegan). The development of religious faith is not our concern; rather, we are concerned with reasons for the adult appropriation of belief in a world with God.

The Introduction to *The World Treasury of Modern Religious Thought* (a useful compendium of recent religious writing) has the comment: "To someone who stands in the tradition of Judeo-Christian monotheism, for example, it may seem obvious that religion presupposes a revelation from the one true and transcendent god (or God), as that revelation has been enshrined in a holy book (or Bible) and main-

---

1. Rodney Stark and Roger Finke, *Acts of Faith: Explaining the Human Side of Religion* (Berkeley: University of California Press, 2000).

tained by a sacred community (or Church)."[2] For anyone closely familiar with the Judeo-Christian Bible and with the teaching of the churches, especially the infallible papacy of the Roman Catholic Church, it should be clear that something more is needed. I was once chatting with a professor of systematic theology at one of the great church universities in Rome. He spoke of the coming semester and I asked what he would be teaching. When he named the course on Revelation, I lit up inside; here was a brain to be picked. So I asked: "Where do you locate the fundamental source of revelation?" His reply, "In the prophets of the Old Testament," left me sadly disappointed; I was certain he knew nothing about them. The follow-up proved me right. So the question is there to be answered: What is the ultimate source of faith in God and, in particular, of Judeo-Christian faith? If not the Bible or the church, then what? The primary revelation of God to us is our experience of the world around us, the basic and original way of knowing God from the beginning of humankind.[3] In Christian faith, the ultimate revelation of God's love for us is God's activity in Jesus Christ, traditionally articulated in terms of the incarnation, Immanuel, God-here-among-us. But heaven help us if we move too fast.

For a lifetime, I have been a committed Roman Catholic; for an academic lifetime, I have been a devoted student of the Older Testament. I know both church and Bible well enough to know that neither can be the ultimate source of faith in God. So, what is? Not the Bible. Not the church. Perhaps the whisper of spirit coupled with the sense of wonder before the insufficiency of experienced reality to account for itself. Unashamedly abstract, but perhaps a beginning.

What will follow, exploring the origins of religious faith — not in the Bible, surprisingly; not from the church, not so surprisingly; not even necessarily from parents, friends, and teachers — is something not many people do too often. Religious faith tends to be instinctive; it is something people live with, take for granted as part of their lives, and seldom explore in its origins. Some are born into lives of religious faith;

2. Jaroslav Pelikan, ed., *The World Treasury of Modern Religious Thought* (Boston: Little, Brown, 1990), p. 3.

3. Cf. Karl Rahner, *Foundations of Christian Faith: An Introduction to the Idea of Christianity* (New York: Crossroad, 1978), esp. Part 2, ch. 2, pp. 51-71; also Part 5, pp. 138-75.

some come to it later in their lives. Without banishing the multiple problems of life, for many of these people faith in God creates a context for living with which they are comfortable; they live and function within a context of faith in God that they find acceptable. Some people, on the other hand, have restless minds that need to explore whatever is available for exploration. Others find the meaning of life an enormous conundrum that demands to be explored. Sometimes, people who for many years have taken their lives and their religious faith for granted come to realize that they want to think it all through. These pages are written for those who at this moment want to explore; for the rest, there is no urgency for such a quest. Buy the book and shelve it.

The Bible

What It Is Not

The Bible is evidence *of* faith in God's being; it is not direct evidence *for* God's being. While it does not contradict the faith-claim of God's existence, it presents options and variants that make it an uncertain witness to the evidence of the past.

There is little doubt that the Bible has had a greater impact on Western European civilization than almost any other book. The extent of its impact has frequently been nearly matched by the extent to which it has been misunderstood. Treated as the revelation of an all-knowing God, it had to be a repository of rectitude, replete with right answers to the questions that troubled human minds. With the Bible offering multiple answers to such questions, choice among them often allowed "experts" to attempt to impose their own convictions in the name of the will of God. More often than answers to questions, the Bible frequently offers an invitation to thought. It is not always couched in terms of invitation. Instead, the invitation may be expressed by juxtaposing differing or contradictory answers. Because the one Bible contains more than one answer to many issues, its readers must think. Like the donkey between two bales of hay, the reader must decide. Serious issues demand serious decisions; hence the invitation to serious thought.

The metaphor of the signpost can illuminate what is meant by the "invitation to thought." If there has been no tampering, one sign pointing in one direction can be most helpful; two signs pointing in two different directions demand further information and invite thought. The longest way round may be the easiest way to the destination; a route that is shorter may also be more difficult. The decision demands reflection; the traveler is invited to thought. The Bible has multiple images of the creation of the world; no single image is revealed. The Bible reader is invited to thought regarding the multiple aspects of the mystery of creation. In Exodus 14, Israel is delivered by crossing the Sea between two miraculously parted walls of water; in the same Exodus 14, Israel is also delivered by staying on one side of the Sea while all night a wind from God miraculously blew the water into the distance, followed at the morning watch by God's panicking the Egyptians so that they fled into the returning sea. Both miracles are interwoven in the one text, inviting thought as to what this means. Israel's time in the wilderness is portrayed in Hosea and Jeremiah as a time of honeymoon fidelity; in the Pentateuch, it is portrayed as a time of stubborn rebelliousness. The Bible reader is invited to thought as to what it means to keep both views. One final example can be taken from the area of divine providence. According to much of Proverbs and Psalms, "the way of the wicked will perish" (Ps 1:6). According to Job, "the wicked are spared in the day of calamity, and are rescued in the day of wrath" (Job 21:30). The Bible reader is invited to thought as to which description of human reality, and God's interaction with it, more closely corresponds with experience and what it means to retain both. The phenomenon is common throughout the biblical text; for examples from major areas, see below.

The Bible's invitation to us to reflect raises a fascinating insight into modern arrogance in biblical interpretation. Wherever traces of an old attitude linger (where the biblical text "accurately described real events and real truths" for its readers and remained "the adequate depiction of the common and inclusive world until the coming of modernity"[4]), it is likely that modern Western arrogance is lurking alongside

4. Hans Frei, *The Eclipse of Biblical Narrative: A Study in Eighteenth and Nineteenth Century Hermeneutics* (New Haven: Yale University Press, 1974), pp. 1, 3-4.

ignorance of modern biblical study. With multiple accounts of creation or flood (see below), the Bible is clearly not presenting an "adequate depiction" of the world. With two miracle stories about Israel's
deliverance at the Sea (Exodus 14), the Bible is clearly not presenting
an "adequate depiction" of what took place. Examples could be multiplied almost endlessly. It is modern arrogance to accuse the Bible of
not being up to the standards of a modern worldview, and so failing to
present a suitably "adequate depiction" of what happened. Given its
plurality (discussed below), the Bible clearly juxtaposes conflicting traditions for a different purpose, a purpose that is *not* that of describing
events in question. Close study shows that the biblical text is not as
naïve as many moderns suppose it to be or would like it to be. It is a
task for modern interpreters to work out what the preservation of such
options might have meant in ancient Israel. A further task for modern
interpreters and theologians is to see how today's people who believe
in a world with God are best supported and nourished in their faith by
such biblical texts.

At some stage, after so many of the biblical narrative texts had been
written, quite probably when offering a base for storytelling yielded to
other functions, other interpretations — midrashic, allegorical, etc. —
were found helpful in providing support for faith in God. Now, we no
longer find them helpful. For example, in most cases an allegorical understanding can no longer be what the text meant in ancient times;
however, that does not invalidate a different use of allegory today — not
what texts might have had as their meaning in ancient times, but what
meaning we might see in them for us today. Our appropriate rejection
of the allegorical, midrashic, etc. does not justify us being blindly historical in our reading when the ancients clearly were not. Instead, we
might look for the symbolic, the theological, and more.

The interpretation of the Bible has made huge progress in the last
few centuries. Equally huge progress remains to be made. A mighty step
in all this was the introduction of the so-called "historical-critical" approach. Unfortunately, by some — perhaps too many — the approach
was understood to be the recovery of history by the use of critical insight. There was no harm in that when it was appropriate. However, a
far more satisfactory, and probably more accurate, understanding of

the historical-critical approach is to see it as the use of critical insight to recognize the historical quality of the biblical text, the historical distance of that text from today, and therefore its demand on critical insight for its interpretation.

A very necessary first stage was to recover what the biblical text might have meant in its own time. "Might have meant" has to be said, because such recovery of meaning is always dependent on the subjective intelligence of the modern interpreter. The idea of recovering "what the author meant" (as opposed to "what the text might have meant") has slowly come to be recognized as, at best, misguided shorthand — unless carefully and wisely nuanced. A key element in this first stage was the emphasis on form criticism, addressing the question: What sort of a text is this? Report? Story? Song? What?

An equally necessary second stage — informed by the first — is to discover what the biblical text, in the light of its past, might mean to us now, in our time. The challenge or invitation is not to see what mysteries we can weave around it. Given an appropriate historical-critical awareness of its situation in the past, the challenge is to see whether, in our changed time, it may still speak to us and "what it might mean" to us.

None of this should undervalue the "word of God." It is fully respectful to scrutinize the biblical word and allow ourselves to be told by it how it is to be understood. Our attitude to this "word of God" is, then, decided by God's word; it is not decided by some inherited past. Just as we discover the nature of this *world* by looking into microscopes and telescopes, so we discover the nature of this *word* by looking into the book with care and respect.

People long to know where they have come from; interest in creation has always been high. It is fateful — perhaps also unfortunate — that the Bible begins on a solemn, sonorous, and most impressive note: "In the beginning, God created the heavens and the earth. . . ." Creation belongs at the beginning; this text is at the beginning; therefore, this must be the truth about creation. Alas, people are too easily satisfied. They do not look at the unfolding of creation in Psalm 104, the delightful description of creation in Proverbs 8:22-31, or the portrayals of creation in Job 26:6-14 or, in words given to God, Job 38:1-38 — and many more. Even right close to hand, people often fail to notice that the creation of our surrounding world is in the background of Genesis 2:4b-25. Allowing the Bible to have its own say on the matter makes adequately clear that Israel believed in creation and, given the various descriptions of it, that Israel did not think it knew how creation had happened. In Genesis One, the massive emphasis on the sequence of six days, with God "sabbathing" on the seventh day, should have alerted readers that more was going on than a simple reflection of creation. The Bible, alas, was not allowed to have its say about itself.

Because, as noted, the Bible often holds together different views, inviting attentive readers to think about the differences, this pattern regarding creation should not be surprising. The Bible may amalgamate views rather than adjudicate between them. It often juxtaposes opposites, without passing judgment. That its readers are slow to learn may be indicative of the level of the readers' needs; it may be indicative of more.

The story of the flood is a case in point. Clearly two substantial accounts are mingled. One centers on 40-day blocks of time, with seven pairs of clean animals and one pair of unclean (and also a final sacrifice), and the floodwaters coming from a great rainstorm; the other centers on 150-day blocks of time, with only one pair of all animals involved (and fortunately no final sacrifice), and the floodwaters coming from the heavens above and the deeps below. If there was a flood, which one was it? Some readers focus on the anger of God, the destruction of sinful humanity, and the deliverance of righteous Noah. The surprises that point to a deeply theological piece are seldom noticed. God is portrayed as grieved, not as angry; in the ten-generation genealogy from Adam to Noah, human sinfulness is hardly to the fore; immediately after the Flood, without allowing for any experience of subsequent human living, human beings are claimed as no different from before (cf. Gen 8:21; 9:2-6). Nevertheless, God is portrayed as committed to human life going on (8:22; 9:1, 7) and as guaranteeing never again to destroy (8:21; 9:8-17). The theological import is massive. The details of any supposed actual Flood are still obscured by the two sets of contenders; in comparison with the theology, the duality is unimportant.

Months after writing the preceding paragraph, I had my attention

53

drawn by Martin Wright, a student at the time, to some fascinating features that need to be developed far more fully than I can dream of doing here. Three elements may be touched on.

First, the account using YHWH (the LORD) begins with the wickedness of humankind, the decision of the LORD to destroy, and no more than a one-verse mention of favored Noah (in all, 6:5-8). Although the presence of the ark in the story implies life after the flood, this aspect is not to the fore — not even in 7:1. After shutting Noah in the ark (7:16), the LORD is not actively present by name in the text until after the sacrifice (8:21); the activity is all Noah's. When the impulses of human wickedness are recalled in 8:21, the description is less drastic than it was at the start; the "every" (כול) and the "only" (רק) and the "continually" (כל-היום) from 6:5 have all been dropped. As portrayed, there is a change in the LORD's attitude from 6:5 to 8:21; the destruction is not to be repeated — despite the absence of significant change in humankind — and life will go on (8:22).

Second, the account using ELOHIM (God) begins, by contrast, emphatically with Noah's righteousness, also listing his sons by name (6:9-10; cf. 9:1, 8), focuses on the corruption of the earth brought about by "all flesh" (instead of the focus on human wickedness), and has God from the outset *explicitly* determined that life on earth will go on, promising to establish a covenant with Noah (6:18). In what follows, the lead figure is God rather than Noah. At the end of it all, as planned, life is to go on, both for every living thing (8:17) and for the human race (9:1). The ideal dispensation of Genesis One is changed to a different dispensation foreshadowing the reality of our world (9:2-6). As portrayed, God's attitude has not changed; God's dispensation has. As a result, the unconditional and everlasting covenant of 9:8-17 is possible.

Third, the present text, resulting from the combination of these two, brilliantly blends the two theologies. Human wickedness is present at the start, but so is the prospect of life continuing. The combination of the two versions widens the initial focus on human evil to include the role of "all flesh" and the corruption of the earth. The LORD's change of heart is preserved, but so is God's change of dispensation. Above all, life goes on without the fear of annihilation. Theologically, the text is immensely rich.

After dealing with humanity, the pattern of retaining opposing views is repeated for the major questions of Israel's origins. On the way out of Egypt, how was Israel delivered at the Sea? As noted earlier, within Exodus 14, two views of the escape from the Egyptian pursuit are to be found: one has Israel crossing the Sea; the other has Israel remaining on one side. Both views are retained. Israel believed it was delivered by God; as to how that deliverance was effected, it clearly did not know.

The time in the wilderness was important for Israel's experience of God. According to Hosea and Jeremiah, it was a time of honeymoon fidelity (e.g., "I will now allure her, and bring her into the wilderness, and speak tenderly to her. There she shall respond as in the days of her youth, as at the time when she came out of the land of Egypt" [Hos 2:17-18, Heb.; NRSV, 2:14-15]). According to the Pentateuch, it was a time of unmitigated rebelliousness (e.g., they "have tested me these ten times and have not obeyed my voice" [Num 14:22]). Both behaviors are part of human living.

The manner of Israel's entry into the land of Canaan is quite unknown. A number of traditions exist, involving kings, soldiers, and sieges and involving miraculous activity by God; no coherent picture emerges from them. Archaeological exploration, even the most recent, does not throw helpful light on the texts.

The emergence of monarchy (= central government) in Israel is portrayed in three different ways: (1) as coming from a demand made by the elders to Samuel for internal justice (cf. 1 Sam 8:4-5); (2) as a spontaneous gift from God for external defense (cf. 1 Sam 9:16); (3) even as Israel's apostasy and infidelity, rejecting God (cf. 1 Sam 8:7-8; 10:18-19). At different times and in different circumstances, kings can be differently viewed. As to how monarchy actually emerged in Israel, we are left entirely in the dark.

On what is probably the greatest question of them all — the issue of human life before God — Psalms and Proverbs say one thing (cf. "the LORD watches over the way of the righteous, but the way of the wicked will perish" [Ps 1:6]); the book of Job says pretty much the opposite (cf. "Have you not asked those who travel the roads, and do you not accept their testimony that the wicked are spared in the day of calamity, and are rescued in the day of wrath?" [21:29-30]); Qohelet ("the Preacher/ Teacher") indulges his skepticism (cf. "all is vanity and a chasing after wind" [Eccl 1:14]).

Even concerning the fate of Israel itself, there is difference. The prophets proclaimed that God would destroy Israel, and Israel was indeed destroyed by Assyrians and Babylonians — its enemies and God's instruments. The same prophets promised that God would restore Israel, and Israel was indeed restored — but hardly as promised.

The upshot of all this: belief in God does not come from the Older Testament; its invitation to think about so many things is not in itself a revelation of God's existence. God's being is taken for granted; it is the background against which discussion and the invitation to thought occur. Of course, there is more to the Bible than the Older Testament, but it is here that Scripture is busy with God and the peoples and their relationships. As a source of information on the reality of God, the Newer Testament is little different from the Older Testament; this is not its role. The resurrection of Jesus Christ is, of course, evidence for the existence of God; but this is not its immediate meaning.

With the Newer Testament, a change of focus rightly takes place that moves from reflection about the experience of God, mediated above all in word and tradition, to the experience of God, immediately present among us in the person of Jesus Christ, experienced as faith in the incarnation of Jesus Christ and as the proclamation of God's kingdom. The focus may change between the Testaments; the nature of the biblical text does not. It is still an invitation to reflection. Without going into other details, three issues stand out, indicating that the text is not a certain witness to the future and does not necessarily provide us with the clarity of knowledge that we need.

1. In the Newer Testament, Christ's Second Coming is spoken of frequently as imminent; but it does not occur and has not occurred. No blueprint there.

2. Slavery is widely endorsed in the Newer Testament, or at least taken for granted. We know better now; in modern Western society, slavery is unacceptable. No early insight there.

3. More significant than anything else: the all-important tension re-

mains unresolved between love and judgment. There are texts in the Newer Testament that strongly affirm the transcendence of God's love and forgiveness over human weakness and frailty; there are texts in the Newer Testament that have God's love and forgiveness inescapably enmeshed in and overcome by the web of human frailty and human freedom. Nothing matters more than the resolution of this tension; the Newer Testament can only be understood as inviting us to reflection. No revelation there.

For all its monotheism, Christianity embraces a plurality (allowing for the Holy Spirit) from which it cannot and should not escape. Jesus Christ, son of God and son of Mary, is God here among us, "utterly us," fully God and fully human. Beyond Jesus, and indeed the Holy Spirit, there is the God who is "utterly other," of whom we cannot speak and should therefore be silent. Jesus-God is utterly human; the one whom we speak of simply as "God" is utterly other. This is not suggesting any dualism in God; it is accepting the difficulty the human mind has in coping with mystery. Good reasons exist, as we will see, to speak of God's being — and little more (at least, on the basis of those good reasons). Good reasons exist to speak of Jesus Christ's life and teaching — and (on the basis of that teaching) so much more. Good reasons exist for accepting that the chasm between the two is not easily bridged by the human mind. Without restriction to Christianity, we humans can speak of a God of creation, whom we can argue about; we can speak of a God concerned about us, whom we simply marvel at (cf. Psalm 8).

Theology should not indulge the temptation to compartmentalize God. God in the Older Testament is deeply involved in human affairs; Jesus-God in the Newer Testament is deeply involved in human existence. The Holy Spirit is deeply involved in human life today. And there, for now, we will leave it.

The Bible has rightly become the word of God. From it, believers extract passages in which they find God speaks to them; it is "word of God." Given the diversity and even the contradictions within it, in its beginnings it is probably more accurate to speak of the Bible as "word of God's people" (see below). Israel spoke of God in many and various ways; the evangelists portrayed Jesus in varying ways. These are most accurately spoken of as words of God's people. Treasured, preserved, and evaluated, they become "word of God" and, as such, should be appropriately understood.

Where Its Value Lies

To say where aspects of the Bible's value lie is not to try and be comprehensive. The value of the Bible to so many people is so vast that it would be foolish to try and encompass it in a chapter or two. Some thoughts may help identify not so much what the Bible's value is but directions pointing to areas where aspects of its richness may be found.

When I was young, the Bible was presented as the record of a time when God was patently evident to people, talking to them and working wonders for them. As my familiarity with the Bible grew, I discovered that the Bible's God was not so very different from the God I encountered in my daily life. Direct communication with God was as uncertain in the Bible as it is today. The wonders of the Bible were often ways of describing faith in the form of stories; they were not so very different from the stories that we can hear from different contexts of faith today. When I was young, the God of the biblical text seemed to me to have been known to those biblical generations rather like the grandparents unknown to me had been known to my mother or father; later, the biblical (OT) text became a reflection on the mystery of God encountered in life then — much as in mine now.

In those days, many of the biblical characters struck me as rather dim-witted, not very bright, uncritically seeing God involved in simple earthly events; all in all, the Bible left as little space for science as, in more recent generations, some science left for God. Closer engagement with the biblical text brought me into contact with biblical authors and editors who were highly intelligent thinkers, very bright lights indeed. My admiration went up by leaps and bounds.

A biblical world not so very different from ours today, inhabited by intelligent if unscientific thinkers, allows respect for the Bible as a foundational document in the life of faith. As discussed above, neither

Older nor Newer Testament serves suitably as *evidence* for the existence of God; they take it for granted. Despite that, both have a foundational role to play in the life of faith.

Older Testament   For many readers, possibly most, the Bible begins with understandably primitive accounts of primitive times: creation, sin, flood, and that sort of thing. It need not be so. Pointers in the biblical text indicate that it may be different.

Where creation is concerned, Genesis One (Gen 1:1–2:4a) is certainly not the one definitive account of how our world came into being. There are too many other accounts of creation in the Older Testament — and they are all different. Israel believed *that* God had created the world; Israel obviously was aware it did not know *how* God had created the world and did not worry about it. There are beautiful creation passages in Proverbs 8:22-31 and Psalm 104, for example; there are many more (see above). Right next door, there is Genesis 2:4b-25. The point of Genesis One is not to provide the definitive account of God's creating; we have to stop and reflect as to what its point might really be. Perhaps an image of the ideal, seen from Israel's point of view.

The story of Adam and Eve is probably not an account of primitive origins either. Actually two stories are skillfully nested together; one, around the tree of the knowledge of good and evil, is told in some detail, while the other, around the tree of life, is no more than hinted at (cf. 2:9; 3:22-24). The names Adam and Eve do not occur in the Hebrew Bible after chapters 3 and 4 (nor do the names of Cain, Abel, and Lamech for example; Noah, later, gets remarkably short shrift [just one reference, Isa 54:9, but important] and Babel does not rate a mention after Gen 11). The genealogy from Adam and Eve through Cain and Abel runs for seven generations to Lamech and his fearful song; then we have a second genealogy, ten generations, from Adam and Eve again, but this time through Seth and Enosh, to Noah and the flood (itself probably the most misunderstood of the Bible's stories). There is even a mini-creation account in Genesis 5:1b-2. Of course, all this can be harmonized into a single narrative (cf. Gen 4:25-26). It need not be; more than that, it probably should not be. Beyond any doubt, there are at least two flood accounts, one with 40-day blocks of time and seven pairs of clean animals, the other with 150-day blocks and only one pair of all animals (see above). The importance of the theological issue embedded in the flood narrative (never again: unconditional coexistence with God) may account for there having been more than one version.

There is much more (some of it touched on above), but that is enough. Instead of primitive accounts of primitive origins, it is highly likely that these opening chapters of the Bible contain significant theological reflections on human life — probably written quite late, naturally placed at the start because they reflect on human life as a whole. Genesis One portrays an ideal world, ordered, structured, obedient to God's commands, oriented from the outset toward sabbath. We humans are in the likeness of God — quite something. The next story (Gen 2–3) is a good example of the human inability not to transgress the boundaries that structure our living. The first story of Cain reflects the human need to cope with inequality (Gen 4:1-16); the second introduces growing civilization (city dwellers, pastoralists, musicians, metalworkers) and the impact of increasing violence (Cain avenged sevenfold, Lamech seventy-sevenfold). The flood stories, beginning and ending with the human capacity for wrongdoing, articulate the belief that life will go on (Gen 8:22; 9:1, 7) and the faith that God will bear with us, will never destroy us in the future (Gen 8:21; 9:8-17) — quite something! The Tower of Babel story (Gen 11:1-9), starting again with a group from the east and a single language, wraps up these opening chapters in an artistic package, returning to much the same theme as Genesis 2–3 (a single group, a similar basic temptation). It is a reminder that after the flood humankind is indeed no better.

Israel had a complex story of its origins and an even more complex picture of how it got to be where it was. In relation to its world, there is blessing to mediate to all the earth (for Abraham: Gen 12:3b; 18:18; 22:18; for Isaac: Gen 26:4b; for Jacob: Gen 28:14b). In relation to its God, there is God dwelling in Israel's midst, surrounded by Israel's tribes, accompanying Israel wherever it was guided (Exod 25–Num 10).

Israel had to work out the meaning of its life with God. So do we in our lives. Faith in God is a delicate creature. Saint Thérèse of Lisieux, a Carmelite nun who died while still young, had deep doubts about God for a year or so before her death. Mother Teresa of Calcutta, founder of the Missionary Sisters of Charity, was troubled by doubt about God from the time she left the Loreto Sisters until her death many years later. The Older Testament is insistent on fidelity to God, an indicator that human life is a constant challenge to belief in God. It is at its most succinct in Isaiah: "If you do not stand firm in faith, you shall not stand at all" (Isa 7:9; NAB: "Unless your faith is firm, you shall not be firm"). Of course, prophets were largely ignored. Little has changed. Imagine a Pope telling a modern President to disarm unilaterally; politically, it would be out of the question.

"Standing firm in faith" is one thing; we all need a good dose of it, whether it is faith in a world without God or faith in a world with God. "Fullness of life" is something else we need a good dose of. The Bible is insistent that faith in God leads to fullness of life. If life is on the lean side, something is wrong with the faith. Clearest for me is the cry early in Jeremiah:

> Be appalled, O heavens, at this,
> > be shocked, be utterly desolate, says the LORD,
> for my people have committed two evils:
> > they have forsaken me, the fountain of living water,
> > and dug out cisterns for themselves, cracked cisterns
> > > that can hold no water.
>
> > > > (Jer 2:12-13)

I need both of those reminders: faith in God as a faith that nourishes life, that is a fountain of living water — not a dry barrenness; cracked cisterns that hold no water, the cisterns I dig for myself, the evanescent goals I set for myself that do not satisfy. The same cry will echo in the Newer Testament: "I came that they may have life, and have it abundantly" (John 10:10).

Quest for a grossly misunderstood fullness of life in a grasping society can often lead to inequality and injustice. The Older Testament, in particular, stands strongly against this. Its conviction echoes again and again in the powerless triad of the ancient world: the widow (husbandless), the orphan (fatherless), and the stranger (without family backup). Faith in God without the struggle for justice in society is a mockery. Isaiah can speak for many:

> Cease to do evil, learn to do good;
> Seek justice:
>> rescue the oppressed,
>> defend the orphan,
>> plead for the widow.

(Isa 1:16-17)

It runs through the prophets of Israel — for example, Amos 5:10-24; Micah 2:1-5; Jeremiah 7:1-15. It is as true today as ever.

With the Bible, Older or Newer Testament, we are far from a God who is "utterly other." The Bible is witness to faith in a God who is wholly engaged with human life. The God who is "utterly other" is the outcome of philosophical thought; the God of the Bible is witness to the fire that faith can kindle in human hearts. The Older Testament constantly calls Israel to commitment in faith to God; it never wavers in its faith in God's commitment to Israel. In the Newer Testament, God's commitment is the core of it all.

One way in which Israel spoke of God's commitment was in the language of covenant. Covenant was the seal put on the God-Israel relationship; Israel's need to observe God's law flowed as a consequence from faith in the reality of that relationship. Another way in which Israel spoke of God's commitment was in the language of love and forgiveness. We will need to explore further the notion of faith in God's love for us (see below). The metaphor of parent and child, yes (e.g., Deut 1:31; Hos 11:1; Isa 49:14-18); even more so, lover and beloved. Israel knew human weakness and our human capacity for wrongdoing; Israel's theologians matched it with God's capacity to love and forgive.

Much of the Older Testament — prophets, narrative books, proverbs, psalms, and so on — can be very hard to follow because it is an amalgam of attempts to reflect on the ups and downs of Israel's experience in terms of a wretched misunderstanding of providence. There are accusations of religious infidelity or social injustice, prophetic menaces of punishment, exhortations to what is right, prayers for deliverance, God's promises for the future, and all that sort of thing. It can get very confusing. The passages are often written for reflection and thought, rather than for public reading. The biblical text can be doubly confusing because it often portrays God as directly involved, and its analysis is based for the most part on the conviction that good deeds are rewarded by God and evil deeds punished by God. If we disagree with this, as some parts of the Bible do, then we will be likely to disagree with some of the Bible's analysis. In the book of Job, this notion of reward and punishment, the dominant view in Israel's thinking — prevalent for example in Psalms and Proverbs — was dismissed as flat wrong (cf. Job 21:29-30). Then as now, the minority opinion (e.g., Job) was just that: a minority opinion. It still is. It can introduce massive confusion into our reading of Older Testament text, especially in terms of Israel's relationship with God. And of course, ours.

Two of my favorite passages speak of God's forgiveness.

From Isaiah:

> I, I am the one
>   who blots out your transgressions for my own sake,
>   and I will not remember your sins.
>
> (Isa 43:25)

From Job:

> If I sin, what do I do to you, you watcher of humanity? . . .
> Why do you not pardon my transgression
>   and take away my iniquity?
>
> (Job 7:20-21)

These are thoughts that create enormous trouble for an unnuanced theology of redemption, a theology in which we are "bought" by the blood of Christ. We have sinned; our world is witness to that. Does a loving God redeem or does a loving God forgive? Theological language should not drive these two apart but work to draw them together. Metaphor is marvelous, as long as our use of it in this context does not lead us astray by diminishing our sense of God's love. Love forgives, and the Older Testament speaks powerfully of God's love for Israel (and by extension, for humankind). For example:

From Hosea:

> The LORD said to me again, "Go, love a woman who has a lover and is an adulteress, just as the LORD loves the people of Israel, though they turn to other gods. . . ." (Hos 3:1)

(To translate from metaphor to plain speech: just as I [God] love Israel, though they don't love me.)

From Isaiah:

> You are precious in my sight,
>   and honored, and I love you.
>
> (Isa 43:4)

These are expressions of Israel's faith. A little further on, we will look at their place in Christian faith.

Love, of course, can go hand in hand with anger; there is plenty of that in the Older Testament. It is important, however, to be clear that we do not — even in the Bible — have access to the inner life of God and God's emotions. What we are given in the Bible are the expressions of human faith in relation to God, to the inner life of God, and to God's emotions. We have access to human faith only. In certain circumstances, how could we not be angry, how could God not be angry? Indignation and anger have their place. If with Israel and us, why not with God?

The real has not always mirrored the ideal. In the history of the real, law has all too often protected property and power more than anything else. In the realm of the ideal, law ought also protect those who have neither property nor power. The grounding image for Israel was of deliverance from Egypt. Individuals and nation had suffered there; individuals and nation had been delivered from there. The powerless, without support for their rights — typified by the triad of widow, orphan, and stranger — were symbols of a nation's justice (see above). God's commitment to a small nation was symbolic of God's commitment to those who believed in God's love. Israel believed that oppression and injustice inflicted on an individual aroused God's anger; Israel's prophets believed that, as a nation, Israel's infidelities and its injustices had aroused God's anger and richly deserved its destruction — or brought about its destruction itself. Much of the language pains us today; many of the circumstances of the time were equivalently painful.

It may seem strange — especially given the fatuous popular differentiation between the God of wrath of the Older Testament and the God of love of the Newer Testament — but Israel's language of God's anger is a pointer to God's involvement with human lives and destinies. The portrayal of a God who is beyond all anger necessarily reflects a God who is beyond concern and beyond love. The God of Jewish and Christian faith cannot be confined to a God who is "utterly other," distant and perhaps unconcerned. Christian faith in the activity of God in Jesus Christ, the incarnation, God's becoming one of us in Jesus Christ, witnesses to God's commitment and concern. The emotions of God, reflected in the Older Testament, are preparation for it. Love and anger go hand in hand. Sin and forgiveness go hand in hand. The Older Testament has much to teach us about life and God.

An aspect that is at the same time both fascinating and troubling is the Older Testament's capacity to respect a distance between belief in divine decisions and their impact on human structures. It is evident in the claims made for the election of Israel's early kings. Saul and David were anointed by Samuel as destined by God to be Israel's kings. Saul was first anointed, and then rejected; David was anointed next to take Saul's place. The divine decisions are there in the early chapters of 1 Samuel (particularly 1 Sam 8–12; 15–16). The impact on the human structures of politics and power takes almost another twenty or more chapters to be finally effective (cf. 1 Sam 16–2 Sam 7). Similarly, at the division of the kingdom, God gives the north to Jeroboam through the prophet Ahijah (1 Kings 11:26-40). The impact on the human structures in the division of the united kingdom into two is attributed to a revolt over taxes (1 Kings 12:1-20). One verse, 1 Kings 12:15, brings the two views into harmony.

Harmony is fine; disharmony is also to be found. The LORD is claimed to have given Jehu high marks and the reward of a four-generation dynasty (2 Kings 10:30). The prophet Hosea expresses a quite different judgment: "I will punish the house of Jehu for the blood of Jezreel" (Hos 1:4). The intermingling of divine and human is seldom simple.

The prophetic promises for the future of Israel are subject to similar problems. Some of the images are superb: "the wolf shall live with the lamb . . . the calf and the lion and the fatling together . . . they will not hurt or destroy on all my holy mountain" (Isa 11:9; cf. 65:25). Alas, not so. "As a mother comforts her child, so I will comfort you; you shall be comforted in Jerusalem" (Isa 66:13). Once again, alas, not so. What the prophets speak of so beautifully is what we rightly believe to be God's longing. What we see before us is what we humans have made of it — a mess. In Israel's imagery, it began in the garden of Eden; it goes on in life. God is believed to long for peace and justice, and we are burdened with so much of the opposite.

The place of prayer in all of this needs noting. Intercessory prayer that begs God to do what faith believes God surely longs to do may, without intending to, downplay our conviction of God's love for us. A far wiser understanding of our prayer is that it gives expression to our own longing for what we believe a loving God also longs for.

Newer Testament The Newer Testament is Christianity's greatest treasure chest, filled with sayings, parables, miracles, and so much more. Just as the Older Testament took God's existence for granted, the Newer Testament takes for granted God's commitment to humankind. It will do us no harm here to explore that commitment a little.

Like the book of Genesis, the gospel according to John gets off to a great start. "In the beginning was the Word, and the Word was with God, and the Word was God. . . . And the Word became flesh and lived among us. . . . No one has ever seen God. It is God the only Son, who is close to the Father's heart, who has made him known" (John 1:1, 14, 18). It is hard to do better than that. The Word was God and the Word became one of us and lived among us — and was scourged and crucified, died and rose from the dead. This may be fact; for us, accepting it is faith.

The sayings are superb; we all have our favorites. The parables have insight and sometimes the kick of a Buddhist koan. What is the sound of one hand clapping? Who is my neighbor? Some people are troubled by the miracles. As always, the question is not what happened, but why was it told and told in this way? Of course there is the question: "Who is this who can do these things?" There are usually overtones involved in the choice of events to tell. So often miracles — healing, peace-bringing, cleansing and community creating, or calming winds or seas or troubles — are stories that point to life. In the context of this little volume, the Newer Testament is an utter treasure because of its witness to God's commitment to us. God's Word became one of us and lived among us.

The hugeness of the God whose creation embraces our 15-billion-year-old universe — perhaps many universes, a multiverse — is utterly beyond our comprehension. We can ask whether such a God exists, and faith replies. We can ask whether such a God could possibly care about us, and the incarnation replies. The Older Testament has the psalmist's exclamation:

> When I look at your heavens, the work of your fingers,
>> the moon and the stars that you have established;
> what are human beings that you are mindful of them,
>> mortals that you care for them?
>
> (Psalm 8:3-4 [Heb., 8:4-5])

The Newer Testament bears witness to more than care: "the Word became flesh and lived among us." Beyond commitment and care, there is incarnation — the sharing of life.

The nature of God's commitment needs exploration. Discussion of love and its universality will have to wait for a couple of chapters. At this point, the question is the priority between redemption and salvation. Faith in God's having become human (the incarnation) places God's commitment to us humans beyond doubt. The question then becomes, to put it with brutal bluntness, whether that commitment is grounded in God's justice or God's love. The ransom of loved ones is, of course, powered by love — love on the part of those effecting the ransom, not those demanding it. Those demanding the ransom may be moved by greed, perhaps by revenge, perhaps by the exercise of power. Whatever it is, it is scarcely love. In the case of God, the only possible power capable of insisting on ransom and redemption would be the claim of God's justice. Otherwise, no power stands over God to demand ransom.

Does it change matters if redemption is substituted for ransom? It can, if our use of language is careful, subtle, nuanced, and fully aware. The payment of a ransom redeems prisoners, releasing them from captivity. Without demeaning God's love, Christians can speak of their redemption when they speak of the reality of Christ's commitment freeing them from captivity to the fear of meaninglessness and the threat of despair. Our becoming fully aware of God's love for us is surely our salvation; aspects of that can validly be spoken of as redemption.

St. Anselm, in a view rooted in the laws of Teutonic tribes, argued that the gravity of offenses was measured by the dignity of the one offended and the worth of atonement by the worth of the one atoning. Only God, therefore, could atone for human failure, could redeem humankind. Anselmian legalism has long been abandoned by theologians; the difficulties it addressed remain. Above all, the suffering and death of Jesus go far beyond anything that an Anselmian system could expect. Moreover as Isaiah and Job remind us, love forgives; love does not seek a ransom. Is God's commitment to humankind grounded in God's love of us? This book answers resoundingly: YES.

Ratzinger highlights the problem involved. After a sympathetic treatment of Anselm, he nevertheless concludes, "It cannot be denied . . . that the perfectly logical divine-cum-human legal system erected by Anselm distorts the perspectives and with its rigid logic can make the image of God appear in a sinister light."[5] Later in the book, he comments: "Many devotional texts actually force one to think that Christian faith in the cross visualises a God whose unrelenting righteousness demanded a human sacrifice, the sacrifice of his own Son, and one turns away in horror from a righteousness whose sinister wrath makes the message of love incredible. This picture is as false as it is widespread."[6]

5. Joseph Ratzinger, *Introduction to Christianity* (London: Search, 1969), p. 174.
6. Ratzinger, *Introduction*, p. 214.

Ratzinger goes on to speak of "man's unqualified 'yes' to God."[7] Faith in God's unconditional love precedes this with the affirmation of God's unqualified "yes" to us — not the cross of Christ as a "yes" to human evil and disorder, but as a "yes" to the value of human life despite its pain. In the Newer Testament, John was right: "We love [God] because he [God] first loved us" (1 John 4:19), taken up by the nineteenth-century English hymn: "I love thee, O thou Lord most high, because thou first hast loved me."

Furthermore, caution is needed, even if we cannot unfold the issue here, because there is a real danger that the notion of atonement will cast a shadow on the meaning of love if the atonement is understood as flowing from love, of course, and so *enabling* forgiveness and releasing love from constraint. Love does not need to be "released" by forgiveness; love embraces forgiveness. Alternatively, atonement that is understood as an expression of forgiving love is surely compatible with the cross and Christian faith. It is in this sense that the ἱλασμὸν — "expiation" or "offering" — of 1 John 4:10 (and of course 1 John 2:2) can be understood.

The issue is central to Christian faith; it is too important not to be reiterated. To quote Ratzinger again: "The expiatory activity by which men hope to conciliate the divinity and to put him in a gracious mood stands at the heart of the history of religion. In the New Testament the situation is almost completely reversed."[8] There, the action is God's not ours: "in Christ God was reconciling the world to himself" (2 Cor 5:19). How is the cross of Jesus Christ to be understood in this context? The full embrace of human life by Jesus in the historical context of his time led inevitably to his death on the cross. Crucifixion was how Romans handled troublemakers. In his time and place, Jesus could not have been seen by the authorities as other than a troublemaker. Had Jesus kept away from Jerusalem at crucial times, he would not have been crucified. His full embrace of human life, however, did not allow him to keep away from Jerusalem at crucial times. In that "full embrace of human life" we see God's love of us, we see God's full embrace of us and

---

7. Ratzinger, *Introduction*, p. 217.
8. Ratzinger, *Introduction*, p. 214.

our lives. The cross of Christ is the ultimate indication that God first loved us (cf. 1 John 4:19).

To give due emphasis to God's love, we are well advised to give priority to the language of salvation over that of redemption — not "to replace" but "to give priority to." Above all, the language of redemption must not be used in ways that threaten to diminish the reality of God's love for us sinners. The most basic significance of the Newer Testament is to cap off the Older Testament's witness to faith in God's involvement with and commitment to us. The whisper of spirit, coupled with our sense of wonder, may point to the reality of a God who is "utterly other." It is a second step, and a radical one, to claim God's commitment to humankind, to us. That is the claim of biblical faith. That is *par excellence* the faith of Christianity with its presentation of Jesus Christ as son of God and son of Mary, crucified and risen from the dead.

Belief that the Creator God should be involved with creation is at the core of Jewish and Christian faith. It is a remarkable leap of faith. For Christians, the incarnation — Jesus as son of God and son of Mary — is Christianity's most traditional expression, its most powerful statement of faith that God is committed to humankind. Whatever language is used, whether redemption and the blood of the lamb or salvation and the love of God, the bottom line is God's commitment.

That this should be almost unbelievable should not surprise us.[9] However, in one form or other, this belief is at the core of Christian faith. "It is impossible to overemphasize the fact that common to the many different ways of thinking is the sense that Jesus came on God's initiative."[10] God's activity on behalf of humankind is believed to have happened because God took the initiative. From this base, belief in God's love for us can unfold. God has moved to be active in Jesus Christ; God is concerned for humankind.

Our interface with the God who is "utterly other" and with the God who is "utterly us" cannot escape from mystery. The more the focus is on the identity of God, the more emphasis needs to be given to the per-

---

9. Cf. the approach taken in *The Myth of God Incarnate*, ed. John Hick (London: SCM, 1977).

10. Frances Young in *The Myth of God Incarnate*, ed. John Hick, p. 18.

fect; the more the focus is on the identity of the human, the more emphasis needs to be given to the less-than-perfect. The mystery is always there. The early centuries of Christianity struggled with the experience and the search for language to express it. Whatever the language, it cannot escape the realm of mystery. Thanks to modern psychology, we have become aware of the mysteries of ourselves and others. Thanks to modern science, we have become aware of the mysteries of the world around us. In such contexts, we can be more comfortable with the place of mystery in our relationships with God.

It may be fair to say that in an overall view of the Newer Testament the consensus is clearly on the activity of God in Jesus. At this stage, focused on the activity of God, an openness is possible to Jewish and Islamic thought. With the passage of generations and continued reflection on experience, in its creedal formulations, Christianity focused on the incarnation (son of God, son of Mary). In the Older Testament, faith in God's commitment to us is a faith primarily expressed in word. In the Newer Testament, faith in God's commitment to us is a faith primarily expressed in a person, in God's activity in Jesus. The differences need not detain us.

It has been said that "the primary importance of Jesus for Christians . . . [resides] . . . in the conviction that he is the one in whom we meet God."[11] For me, the primary importance of Jesus is that he is the one in whom God meets us. The metaphysics matter; however, they can be left to metaphysicians. Faith in Jesus as vessel of God's activity (focused: incarnate son of God) is faith in God's commitment to humankind. The Older Testament expresses faith in God's commitment to humankind, strongly affirmed at Genesis 8:21-22 and 9:1, 7 — and many other places. Following on the Newer Testament, faith in the incarnation gives that commitment the reality of an individual person — the Word become flesh.

The full reality of faith in Jesus Christ as God-become-human can only be accounted for either by dismissing it as the product of religiously fevered human imagination, a divine man of the legendary and mythic realm, or by accepting it as faith in the expression of God's com-

---

11. Maurice Wiles in *The Myth of God Incarnate,* ed. John Hick, p. 8.

mitment to the humankind that has emerged on our earth, a commitment that may best be articulated in terms of love. No other terms serve as well.

The sheer humanness of Jesus should not be overlooked, beyond sayings, parables, miracles, and such. Like others of his time, Jesus traveled on foot between Galilee and Jerusalem. Unlike others of his time, Jesus apparently had no house and family to call his own. He mixed with common Galilean fisherfolk, not the privileged and powerful of this world. Among his close friends and disciples, he picked a dud (Judas Iscariot) — or he took a risk. In the garden of Gethsemane, before the prospect of arrest, trial, and crucifixion, he felt sheer fear. Like other religious-minded people, he communed with God in prayer. In so many ways, the fullness of his humanity emerges from the pages of the Newer Testament portrayal.

As background, available for the confirming of Christian faith, there is belief in the reality of a god, grounded in the whisper of spirit and the sense of wonder, and there is belief in this god's concern for and commitment to humankind, traditionally grounded in the incarnation and resurrection of Jesus Christ, son of God and son of Mary.

It is a faith that leads to life and love, to community and justice within that community, within society. In the words given Jesus: "I have come that they may have life and have it abundantly" (John 10:10). What is life without love? "There will be one flock, one shepherd" (John 10:16). Within that one flock, loved by that one shepherd, there can be no place for social injustice; Matthew appeals to Isaiah for the image of Jesus: "He will not break a bruised reed or quench a smoldering wick until he brings justice to victory" (Matt 12:20). John takes a different tack. "Unless a grain of wheat falls into the earth and dies, it remains just a single grain; but if it dies, it bears much fruit" (John 12:24): the saying speaks of Jesus; it speaks of human life and has its meaning for the lives of all of us. "No one has greater love than this, to lay down their life for friends" (John 15:13). If we wonder about the extent of that "friends" — is it perhaps restricted to a privileged few? — its universality is spelled out for us; God first loved us (1 John 4:19). Loved by God, we are friends; exclusiveness is absurd.

The Church

What It Is Not

Henry Ford may not have been right to dismiss history as "bunk," but he instinctively knew that to many people it was not of great interest. So we will dispense with a short course of European church history here. The revelation of God's existence is not enshrined in the Bible; that we have seen. Instead, *faith* in God's existence is to be found there. The question now is whether some such revelation has been "maintained by a sacred community (or church)" (see the start of this chapter). A short course of European church history would respond with a rather resounding No.

The community of those who believe in God can be a powerful force for faith in God. A wealth of intelligence and a wealth of good works are hard to ignore, although they can be balanced by a plethora of ignorance and superstition, fear and folly, or just plain mixed motives and vested interests. If we turn from the better aspects of the community of believers to look to its institutional leadership, the outlook is not always rosy for maintaining a faith in God. In Europe at least, church history over the centuries is far from universally edifying; it tells all too often a story of struggles to maintain power in society. It reveals the very human side of the institutional churches, not in itself a bad thing. Unfortunately, this "human side" is too often tainted with greed for money, ambition for power, and lust for social prestige.

Few institutions escape such flaws; few institutional churches either. If we are to reflect on this briefly, in assessing the sources of faith in God, as a Roman Catholic I will restrict my emphasis to the flaws in my own church. Others can reflect on their own; criticism from within is often more appropriate. For churches as for faiths, one needs to have lived deeply within it in order legitimately to criticize.

The issue of usury is an old one. Quite simply, the Roman church, like plenty of others at the time, did not understand the nature of money. The issue of slavery cuts very close to the bone. It is right through the Bible, Older and Newer Testament. "Wives, be subject to your husbands, as is fitting in the Lord. . . . Slaves, obey your earthly masters in everything . . . fearing the Lord" (Col 3:18, 22). According to family tradition, my great-grandfather was the last man in Scotland legally to own a slave. That is far too close to home. Until recently, the churches gave little leadership on the issue. Given this sort of background, I am not disposed to find in the churches a source for belief in a world with God.

Within the Roman Catholic communion, one can hardly speak of church authority today and not mention papal infallibility. When immersed in the broad concerns of a theology of church, the issue of the continuance of right thinking is of immense importance. When reduced to an in-house struggle for the balance of power, the infallibility issue is vastly less significant. As one editor wrote: "Growing around the edges of the infallibility debate is a suspicion that the whole affair is a pseudo event. . . . For every breath of suspicion, however, there are two of disinterest. 'So what!'"[12] The debate about infallibility ended up in the closing decades of the twentieth century being conducted in the narrow terms of what seems now a cross between careerism and a media beat-up. It purported to center on the issue of papal infallibility but more important issues were involved — above all, central authority. Hans Küng writes that "we shall never understand the definition of papal infallibility merely by analyzing the text of the Council's Constitution in Denzinger's *Enchiridion*. . . . The issue was largely decided before the Council met."[13] Within its context, that is true, but papal infallibility today relies on an implicit appeal to the definition of infallibility at Vatican I in 1870. So the definition cannot be ignored — and it claims very little. Küng again: "the formula finally agreed on . . . fell far short of the original ideas."[14] That formula, however, is what was defined by the Council. Authority may claim to rest on it, but far better grounds for authority can be found. Infallibility in itself is a remarkably weak reed.

For all the rhetoric written about it, papal infallibility is a remarkably good example of modern ecclesiastical politics; it hardly has doctrine at its core. It is a classic example of the situation — not unknown in church politics — where a universal council has declared one thing and the authorities of the church have assiduously proclaimed some-

12. John J. Kirvan, ed., *The Infallibility Debate* (New York: Paulist, 1971), p. v.
13. Hans Küng, *Infallible? An Enquiry* (London: Collins, 1971), p. 73.
14. Küng, *Infallible*, p. 80.

thing stronger (cf. the restraint of the Council of Trent on Scripture and Tradition ["*both* in Scripture *and* in Tradition"] and the exaggeration of later church proclamation ["*partly* in Scripture and *partly* in Tradition"]). The limits placed on infallibility were clear and known to informed Roman Catholics at the time and since. Papal infallibility applied only when the Pope was speaking "ex cathedra," that is, as pastor and teacher of all Christians, addressing the whole church, and speaking of doctrine concerning faith or morals. As spelled out in the definition, what papal infallibility involved on such an occasion is seldom talked about; it wasn't and isn't much.

According to the definition, the Pope, under these specific conditions, enjoyed that infallibility which the divine Redeemer wanted his church to enjoy when defining doctrine concerning faith or morals.[15] At once the political drift is clear: the Pope is given a personal authority balancing that of the universal councils. The claim is carefully and minimally phrased: that infallibility which the divine Redeemer wanted his church to enjoy. Many Newer Testament scholars have grave doubts whether Jesus wanted to lay down structures and institutions for a church. Many church historians have grave doubts about the history of the church as witness to its infallibility.

Defined in 1870 and invoked once for the definition of the Assumption in 1950, papal infallibility as a doctrine of the Roman Catholic Church has been much trumpeted and little used. Use might bring attention to bear on its fragility. Interestingly, a recent papal declaration rejecting the priestly ordination of women, and touted as potentially infallible, obliged people *definitively to believe;* it did not indicate a commitment on the part of the Pope *definitively to teach* — significant, given the meticulous care involved in formulating pontifical documents. Small wonder. Pontifical theologians had reason enough to be cautious with the document's claims. Among the doctrines of the Roman church, infallibility is a latecomer; its doctrinal significance is unlikely to be large.

---

15. Henricus Denzinger and Adolfus Schönmetzer, *Enchiridion Symbolorum: Definitionum et Declarationum de Rebus Fidei et Morum,* 22nd ed. (Freiburg im Breisgau: Herder, 1963), §3074.

In my own profession as a Scripture scholar and in my theological training as a Roman Catholic priest, two issues stand out as particularly painful for me.

The first is a pontifical decision of 1906. It had all the weight of papal infallibility invested in it — and it was wrong. The upsurge in critical biblical scholarship toward the end of the nineteenth century, led in the main by Protestant Germany, caused problems for the authority of the Scriptures and consternation at Rome. A Pontifical Biblical Commission was set up and its decisions given a force equivalent to that of papal infallibility. The Commission was asked whether adequate evidence existed to justify the conclusion that Moses had not written the Pentateuch. The Commission's response was that such evidence did not exist. The response was wrong; such evidence did exist at that time. It is now almost universally acknowledged. What was quite right, and should have been said, was that Roman Catholic biblical scholars and theologians had difficulty integrating these views into their faith. Today, these views can be integrated into faith and so they are widely accepted. The irony is that, while Mosaic authorship of the Pentateuch is still dismissed by most, the hypotheses that surrounded the issue are now largely open to debate and doubt.

When the evidence stares you in the face, wrong claims are hard to whitewash. For example: you are told that if a pot of water is put on a stove, it will not boil; you put the pot on the stove and the water boils. You know that what you were told was wrong. I knew that what I was told about Moses and the Pentateuch was wrong.

The second issue is the papal encyclical on birth control, "Humanae Vitae." It was issued in 1968, a year after I was ordained to the priesthood. A respected insider has claimed that the bulk of it was written by one of my professors of theology. This man was available for the two years involved. His theology was coherent with much that is good in the encyclical; what is not would not have come from him. Encyclicals seldom get written by a single author. As is well known, the encyclical was preceded by a long period of uncertainty, in which different moral theologians proposed different approaches and different conclusions. Following that decade or so, a broadly based papal commission was established to advise the Pope. The commission is reported to have advised a wisely nuanced position favorable to contraception. Some few (among them allegedly Karol Wojtyla, subsequently Pope John Paul II) are reputed to have convinced the Pope to endorse the contrary view, unfavorable to contraception. My primary complaint is not that the encyclical was wrong; my primary complaint is that, in issuing it in the way it did, my church was dishonest. Years of uncertainty, the convoking of a commission and its deliberations, were not followed by the admission of difficulty and the advocacy of a prudential decision on the part of the authority of the Roman Catholic Church. To the contrary, alas, the encyclical gave the impression of claiming the clarity and authority of eternal truth. That claim was dishonest.

Papal documents come and go. Some among us remember "Veterum Sapientia," a papal document of the highest authority *(motu proprio)* signed on the high altar of St. Peter's by none other than the much-loved Pope John XXIII. It stipulated that ecclesial studies throughout the Roman church be taught in Latin. It was a dead letter before it was signed. Quite to the contrary, "Humanae Vitae" has been far from a dead letter. It has not changed the moral convictions of most Roman Catholics; it has massively affected papal authority — probably a good thing. In its day, it caused enormous suffering, mainly to faithful women — a source of great grief and regret. Why "Veterum Sapientia" should have been so easily ignored and "Humanae Vitae" taken so seriously is a matter for anguished reflection. Perhaps "Veterum Sapientia" *directly* affected only clerical academics (seminary teachers, etc.), while "Humanae Vitae" *directly* affected married couples and had an impact only *obliquely* on celibate clergy. This difference probably played a role; equally, it is probably not the whole story.

Painful as it may be, for me therefore — discounting many other things — one Roman decision was wrong and another dishonest. I can hardly source my faith in a world with God to the authority of my church.

Where Its Value Lies

Much as we said earlier about the Bible, it would be foolish to try and spell out a comprehensive picture of the values of the church. It means too many things to too many people. It helps, however, to point out certain directions where aspects of those values lie.

Unity is the aim of the ecumenical movement; unity is an imperative for Christian churches. Over and above that, unity in leadership and visibility is of value to Christian faith. The Church of England has its primacy in the see of Canterbury. The Church of Rome has its primacy in the Vatican. Others give expression to primacy in other ways. And others again abhor it.

In a developed world that is massively materialist in its thinking and its living, its politics and its power, a unified voice articulating the whisper of spirit is desperately needed, speaking out for the values of Christian faith — others, especially Jews who share so much of our biblical faith, will please understand that I write of Christian faith because I know it from within; that, naturally, I cannot say of other faiths. Beyond this, there is the reality that unity among believers in a world with God can be a support for Christian faith. The awareness that one's understanding of the world is shared with others, whether on a global scale or in the relatively small local community, can be a source of support.

Unity is delicate and fragile. At a global level, it needs to embrace an enormous breadth of interests: widely differing countries and cultures; widely differing concerns, from the conservative to the liberal; widely differing interpretations of power and position. At the local level, there are the differences of individuals, in their beliefs and in their needs. There are regional differences within countries; there are gaping cultural differences between countries. Regional differences can be vast; cultural differences are vaster. China, India, Africa, Europe, North and South America — and more.

Extent is not the only difficulty to beset the visibility of unity. In today's world, conformity to religious leadership can hardly be coerced. Once upon a time, the condemned could be publicly executed, heretics burned, or dissenters otherwise punished. Now, loyalty to leaders must be earned and the right to dissent cannot be withdrawn. Once upon a time, public opinion could be controlled from above; in the age of the Internet and the World Wide Web, the same public opinion is not easily suppressed. U.S. President Harry Truman is reputed to have told a deputation from the Daughters of the American Revolution: "Ladies, you have convinced me; that was the easy part of your task. Now you must get out there and generate the political pressure that obliges me to do it." It is no longer enough for the wise in authority to command; they must persuade — and, in politics, be persuaded (by the voters).

Various churches had their various ways of coercing compliance with authority. Once upon a time, Rome's adherents believed their eternal salvation could be endangered. That time has passed. If authority and leadership are effective today, in all churches as a rule it is for reasons other than fear. For those "subject to authority," putting aside issues of promotion and peer pressure, etc., truly soul-destroying fear is seldom to be reckoned with. Ostracism is still possible; burning at the stake (or equivalent) is no longer possible. Once the saying in Roman Catholic circles was: Rome has spoken; the matter is decided ("Roma locuta est; causa finita est"). Now, the saying is rather: Rome has spoken; the matter may be worth discussing. The benefit is huge; those exercising authority, seeking to exercise leadership, can only do it by appealing to hearts and minds. There is much to be said for that.

Various churches had various ways of handling ecclesial authority when it overstepped its bounds. The Roman church gave what is called the issue of "reception" attentive study. If a decision was not "received" by church members around the world, it was left in abeyance. Authorities, of course, did not like the idea; theologians and canon lawyers smiled on it. The classic example in recent years has been "Veterum Sapientia" (noted above) — a dead letter from Day One.

Faith is a fragile flower, whether faith in a world with God or in a world without God. Within the routine of human living, the very fragility of faith, above all faith in a world with God, intensifies the need for community support and a degree of global visibility. The sense of spirit within us and the sense of wonder before all that is in and around us are whispers; they are not hammered home by the media and they do not force themselves into our faces ("whispers": in Karen Armstrong's words, "a moment of truth . . . this momentary illumination . . . that moment of inarticulate longing" which we cannot recapture).[16] They can

---

16. Karen Armstrong, *A History of God. From Abraham to the Present: The 4000-Year Quest for God* (London: Heinemann [Mandarin Paperbacks], 1993), pp. 142-43.

be ignored; they can be brushed aside. They can make claims that seem impossible. It helps to have them confirmed by the experience of others, by the insights of gifted people, by the awareness that — flawed and tainted though so much religiosity may be — faith in a world with God is significantly shared.

"Significantly shared" sounds pompous and empty. But art and music, architecture and sculpture, liturgical expression and symbol are significant, can be shared, and can be at the service of religious faith. When these are coupled with full human lives, with wisdom and learning, they can generate a groundswell in support of religious faith that is not negligible. Visibility differs from the close-knit village to the global media; unity differs from the local to the global. At every point, a contribution can be made and the insights of religious faith can be confirmed.

Can all this confirmation add up to certitude? Perhaps for some; for many, assuredly not. Can aspects of the religious faith of some be a source of trouble and disquiet for others? Assuredly so. Can the religious faith of many, for all its flaws, be a source of strength and confirmation for many? Assuredly yes.

At the local level, what can be most destructive of unity is the power-struggle. The unity of belief may not suffer; the unity of believers often does. At the global level, difficulties for unity and leadership multiply, rabbit-like. The Vatican's mastery of the world's media can only be admired and envied. The Vatican's mastery of the art of obscurantism is less admirable and can be regrettably baneful. The glare of publicity can illumine the fineness of spirit; it can also focus the spotlight on folly.

The overwhelming preeminence of the Vatican's public image is a major plus and a major problem. There is unquestionably the media preference for an individual over a committee or even a committee chair. The very fact of the latter — individual but tied to the authority of the committee — brings home an aspect of the problem. It may not be so much that the Pope is an individual with vast authority; to the contrary, it may be that the vast authority comes from sources that can be tainted. It is the sainted status of the individual that causes problems: the perception of almost unfettered church authority, the aura of sanctity ("Your Holiness"), the belief in a closeness to God. It can be hugely beneficial; it can be correspondingly dangerous.

The difficulty bedeviling accepted leadership in the realm of religious faith today is one of its being compartmentalized within specific churches, denominations, or faith communities. As a result, rather than any single individual or any single office, a number of heads need to be involved, respectful of one another, embodying for those who share their faith something of its respectability. Beyond "specific churches, denominations, or faith communities," in many nations and cultures, faith in a world with God may extend more widely than simply Christian faith.

The respectability will be real only if there is respect for each other and even more respect for each other's faith and culture. Individuality is evident and desirable at the personal level; it is similarly evident and desirable at the cultural and national level. The respectability of Christian leadership can be significant as witness to faith in a world with God, especially when it demonstrates the breadth to embrace both what may be common and what is different. Certain core aspects of Christian faith are shared among many Christian leaders: first and foremost, belief in the reality of God and God's love for us; beyond that, belief in the incarnation (God's presence in a human person, living a fully human life through to its end), the crucifixion, death, and resurrection of Jesus Christ, and of course its continuation in the eucharist. Even within these core elements there are differences: subtler differences on the understanding of God; more radical differences on issues of incarnation, resurrection, and eucharist.

For Christians, such differences can well be chasms on the landscape of faith in a world with God. What should not be overlooked is that, although they are chasms on the landscape, they are witness to the presence of the landscape. It is not so surprising that there are chasms; it is surprisingly assuring that there is a landscape. The whispers are not loud enough to enable us to make out the contours of a landscape without doubt. The whispers are audible enough to allow for the possibility of some such landscape. That in itself is something.

No one voice dominates others in the articulation of whisper. In the ideal order, at least, authority is based on respect; respect is given where deserved. Respected authority is tempered by reality. Influences from reality include issues of distance and of attitude.

A major difference is that between center and periphery. This is not solely a matter of geography; attitude can matter as much as distance. The psychological periphery can be located at the geographical center. It can be; it need not be. In matters of authority, center and periphery have different roles to play. In any system, it is of the essence of the center's role to give guidance and seek to rein in excess; it is of the essence of the periphery's role to push against the restraints of the center. Only in the tension generated is life to be found rather than stagnation. There are those, in so many circumstances, who need a leadership without fallibility or flaw. There are those, especially among the cynics, who all too automatically clothe leadership in fallibility and flaw. The middle ground can be elusive.

In individual life, "growing pains" are taken for granted; living pains and dying pains are spoken of less frequently, but they are there. In institutional life, all these areas of pain are permanently present. Just as growing pains are a sign of life, these pains in an institution are a sure sign that the institution has not yet withered on the vine. The more rigidly demanding authority is, the more likely it is to insist that its guidance be followed and the more likely the periphery is to resent and resist such restraint. If this is recognized as inherent in systems management, the hurt will not go away but it may be to some degree diminished.

One of the permanent risks that endangers any central authority is the confusion of leadership with power. Invariably, one-sided focus on the preservation of power leads to the stifling of innovation and a clinging to the familiar that ends up in obscurantism. Beyond that, the struggle to preserve power can erode people's faith and stop their ears to the whisper of spirit. The reverse, of course, is risk of the periphery's attachment to what may be seen as political correctness and the endorsement of ephemeral fads. For a healthy institution, life flows from the tension between these two, between center and periphery.

The "periphery" often consists of specialists and those who work with them; for example, interpreters of Scripture, thinkers and theologians, those involved in the everyday pastoral life of their church. Specialists work under the attraction and control of features of their field that are specific aspects of life. Exegetes (specialists of Scripture) are drawn by the experience of biblical text, the experience of people's lives, and the faith tradition of their church. Theologians are drawn by their experience of faith in God, their reflection on the history of thought, their experience of people's lives, and the faith tradition of their church. Those involved in the pastoral life of the church are impelled by the impact of the functioning of the church on the lives of people, the input into this of scholars and other specialists, and of course the faith tradition of their church. The description is far from exhaustive; it will do as a beginning. At the "center," on the other hand, are those whose major concern, like it or not, is the faith tradition of their church, but who are not subject to the same input from people's lives, from experience of the biblical text, or from exposure to the history of thought. They are concerned to see how the moves and claims being made on the periphery fit into the advance of the faith tradition of their church.

This is not a matter of conservatives and liberals. Both are found at the periphery; both are found at the center. It is a matter of perspectives and pressures. The perspective of the center is primarily the whole; the perspective of the periphery is normally the local. The pressures at the center reflect the dynamism of a vast institution. The pressures at the periphery come from biblical text, theological thought, liturgical practice, and the encounter with the lives of believing people ("the faithful"). Regional differences are but one aspect to be taken into account. What may be necessary in France or Germany may be unthinkable in Venezuela or Brazil; what may be highly desirable in central Europe may be anathema in sub-Saharan Africa. The center probably finds the periphery a pain, but many believe new life is more likely to begin with the periphery rather than the center. The periphery probably finds the center a pain, but continuity and fidelity are likely to be strong at the center. Tension between the two is indicative of life; it is to be expected.

Christian institutions tend to seek the sinless. Where leadership is concerned, they might be wise to recognize with Lord Acton (a distinguished nineteenth-century historian) that great men are seldom good men. Given that Acton was writing in the context of the Roman papacy, with due allowance for exceptions, the next step is legitimate: great popes are seldom good. Simon Pure we cannot have; we have to settle for Simon Peter — impetuous, scared, and a symbol of hope for us all.

The search for the "Simon Pure" will certainly fail; the search for good leadership should go on.

No Jewish or Christian organization has discovered the ideal. Variations have been tried at various levels and in various ways: the local parish, church, or synagogue; the regional presbyteries, deaneries, dioceses, and the like; even Primates, Patriarchs, and Popes, Canterburys, Vaticans, Rabbinates; and bodies like the World Council of Churches. Nothing is perfect; nothing is likely to be. It is probably unthinkable, but it would be wonderful if the leaders of the great groupings of Jews and Christians — and, when or where appropriate, Islam and others — could reach one another on issues central to faith in God and God's relationship to humankind. Committees meet today to push forward issues of union between churches or relationships between specific groups. Faith in God, however, in a world that needs such faith and is drifting from it, is not adequately addressed. It needs to be.

An unpleasant crisis is brewing unless the leaders of Christian faith worldwide put their heads together and place the origins and meaning of Christian faith on a secure base, a base that is not grounded in a misrepresentation of the Bible (see below). Should Christian churches cling to misrepresentation, resulting in a catastrophic storm of worldwide dimensions, the leaders of such churches will have no one but themselves to blame. Ecumenical infallibility may be an amusing image and little more; ecumenical intelligence and leadership may be unlikely, but it should not be beyond our dreams. If rabbis and imams can meet, why should not Christians join them?

St. Paul wrote to the Corinthians about a faith that rested "not on human wisdom but on the power of God" (1 Cor 2:5). The "power of God" can be experienced or symbolized in many ways. Christian faith may not rest on "human wisdom," but a little wisdom from the leaders of Christian churches would go a long way.

An Aside

The distinction between the hierarchy and bureaucracy of a church and the church itself is of the greatest importance. I can make it emphatically for the Roman Catholic Church; others can make the distinctions for their own churches. In the Roman Catholic Church, it might be termed the "FBR" (the Fallible Bureaucracy of Rome). A bureaucracy of some sort may be necessary for running a church; it may not be helpful for discerning truth. The FBR must never be confused with what is termed "the church." The church is made up of all its human members, from the most exalted Pope to the most recent newborn. The FBR would like it to be different; "the church" should never let "them" get away with it.

EXCURSUS
God's Word, God's People, Word of God's People

Christian faith's involvement with the evolution of the modern world probably stretches at least from the Reformation to the Second Vatican Council. Interwoven with this has been a larger issue than involvement with the perceptions of a changing world. The issue: the understanding of Bible as God's word.

As the nineteenth century turned into the twentieth, the Roman Catholic Church threw the weight of its teaching authority against contemporary trends in biblical studies. It proved to be wrong. As the twentieth century has turned into the twenty-first, acceptance of trends in biblical studies is likely to undermine certain façades of Christian faith.

Critical reading of the Older Testament goes back at least to Baruch Spinoza, Dutch philosopher and Jewish scholar (1632-77). As an academic discipline, critical biblical study was in full swing in the nineteenth century. Its impetus owed much to Martin Luther's understanding of the place of Scripture in Christian faith: Scripture dominated ("sola scriptura," Scripture alone); tradition diminished. The Roman church had tried to limit the impact of Scripture by appeal to what could be put under the heading of tradition. For many, critical study of the word of God helped balance the weight given to tradition. From the pious point of view, the closer one studied the Bible, the closer one came to God.

Probably a confluence of factors have had their impact on biblical studies in Western Europe. The increasing decline of religious faith in Europe, as elsewhere in the West, has to play its role. The high level of technicality in biblical studies, excluding many, has its role to play. The perceived irrelevance, not to say threat, of the outcome of so much biblical study will also have contributed. There is a perception that many biblical scholars are retreating into the academic world and that, often, academic study does not fuel and foster religious faith. In blunt terms: academic biblical study for the last couple of centuries has been contributing to the gradual erosion of the foundations of the biblically based churches.

At the turn from nineteenth to twentieth century, the Roman church was coming to terms slowly and painfully with the modern world. Much was changing: monarchies to democracies, class and privilege based on birth to class and privilege based on wealth, agricultural society to industrial society, and so on. Resistance to critical exploration of the Bible may have been wrong, but it is understandable. Within the Roman Catholic communion, the foremost proponents of such critical exploration of the Bible did not seem able to integrate the results of their studies with their faith. So it seemed that faith was threatened. Condemnation and rejection held the line until the threat to faith was removed and the 1943 encyclical, "Divino Afflante Spiritu," gave papal blessing to critical study of the Bible.

Religious faith survived. Belief in the Bible as source of God's guidance, wisdom, and revelation remained. The writings of the Newer Testament and the lives of Christians are the only witnesses to what found expression as faith in the incarnation, death, and resurrection of Jesus Christ. That is beyond doubt. In my professional judgment, as an Older Testament scholar and as a faithful Roman Catholic priest, what is in doubt is whether the Bible can any longer be considered in faith as the revealing gift of God's guidance, wisdom, and revelation. The seven major areas discussed earlier have their impact here: creation (multiple texts), flood (at least dual texts), Sea (at least dual), wilderness (dual), occupation of the land (at least dual), monarchy (triple), and providence (dual). (For details see Chapter 3, pp. 52-56 — and these are only the majors!) Given such diversity, we can speak of invitation to thought; we can hardly speak of revelation or instruction. Of course we can choose between them — and we do. Whether we like it or not, the reality of what is called a "canon within the canon" is out there (advocated academically above all by Ernst Käsemann[17]). Selected Scriptures are attended to (Käsemann: seen as Gospel) while other Scriptures are set aside (Käsemann: seen as Law). Such selectivity is part of the everyday reality of church life, but there are difficulties. First, this option sets human choice and authority over the word of God, rather than the other way round. Second, the idea of a canon within the canon that is "permanently reformable" (i.e., open to revision) is an inadequate response. Precisely as "canon," it is claiming for the humanly chosen biblical text an authority that, as humanly chosen, it cannot have. Such biblical text is not humanly recognized divine guidance, wisdom, and revelation; it is the reflection of God's people, humanly recognized as helpful and appropriate to present circumstances.

After a lifetime spent involved in biblical scholarship, this understanding expresses for me the outcome that the biblical text itself has led many to recognize. What we have long revered as word of God remains word of God — but selectively, for the user (i.e., what is selected by a user as speaking truly would indeed be "word of God" to that user — without needing appeal to academic authority). Taken totally, despite the ardent faith of our evangelical sisters and brothers, the biblical word may be best understood as word of God's people, a word that invites us to reflection. Through their writing, under the power of the Holy Spirit, the biblical authors articulate their faith in God in the light of their experience of life. The importance given to their finding God for themselves balances the importance of God's revealing God to them. We who come after them, also under the power of the Spirit, may find in this articulation what speaks to us truly of God.

The Bible (both Older Testament and Newer Testament) is the word that God's people wrote down for themselves, and for those to come after them, so that from it the word of God might be addressed to them and to those who came after them — including us. Many of those who are intimately involved with scriptural text have reached their own un-

17. Ernst Käsemann, *New Testament Questions of Today* (London: SCM, 1969), ch. 14, pp. 260-85.

derstanding of how precisely it is to be regarded. "Word of God's people" is one such possibility. From earliest times, there have been many ways of approaching Scripture. Honesty requires words that are least open to misunderstanding. Hence, "word of God's people."

Another way of putting this is to assess whether it is more appropriate to describe the Bible as the word God addresses to us or as the word God preserves for us — "addresses" for our instruction or enlightenment, "preserves" for our reflection or thought. The issue is one of assessing what is most accurate and least subject to misunderstanding in describing the biblical text we have received.

A pointer to one aspect of what is meant may be taken from a recent learned commentary on one of the Older Testament biblical books. The author wrote: "the covenant is not revoked and the promise remains unbroken throughout all generations." What the author unquestionably meant was: "Israel's faith continued in the belief that the covenant is not revoked and that the promise remains unbroken throughout all generations." God did not make the covenant; Israel's theologians believed the language of covenant was an appropriate way to express faith in the God-Israel relationship. God did not make the promise; Israel's theologians believed it was an appropriate expression of faith in the God-Israel relationship. Honesty and accuracy demand that faith, once upon a time implicit, must today be given explicit acknowledgment.

As word of God's people, the Older Testament is witness to a faith in God's closeness to and commitment to Israel and all humankind. As word of God's people, the Newer Testament is witness to a faith in God's activity in Jesus — the life, death, and resurrection of Jesus Christ — understood in due course as a faith in the incarnation, God's becoming a human being. As word of God's people, the Bible is a precious resource in traditional areas where it has always served.

When approaching the Bible spiritually, for reading and prayer rather than study, the Bible is wonderful for arousing feeling in us, for fueling religious faith, for firing imagination. When approaching the Bible more critically, for study rather than reading or prayer, the Bible is revelatory of faith in a God committed to humankind (OT), a God who has become part of humankind (NT); the Bible is marvelous for probing the foundational base of much religious faith; the Bible has an unsettling knack for challenging our understanding of ourselves. For many, reading in the Bible is a familiar occasion for hearing the whisper of spirit.

What the Bible does not do and should not be asked to do is to provide God's self-revelation and disclosure of God's will. The Bible is the product of reflection on faith, faith seeking to understand the meaning of life before God. The Bible is not a source of direct divine guidance, nor does it offer direct access to the divine will. It offers reflections from within the standpoint of religious faith and, where these reflections differ among themselves, it invites the believer to further reflection and choice.

Recent developments, over the past fifty years or so, suggest that the moves which will sideline the Bible as a source of divine guidance, a sure expression of the divine will, may have their impact over the next fifty to a hundred years. Already, among the powerhouses of biblical studies, from a methodological point of view, Germany is becoming increasingly isolated and irrelevant; America is embracing issues that are important in themselves but may prove ephemeral for biblical studies. Academically, the churches are in trouble. In the decision-making sphere, recently enough in the worldwide Anglican communion, the bias of the bishops regarding homosexuality was blamed on the Bible. Hardly fair to the Bible! Recently enough in the worldwide Roman communion, the folly and fear of frightened old men regarding women's role in worship was blamed on the Bible. Hardly fair to the Bible!

CHAPTER 4

Contribution of Whisper

An Ultimate Origin for Faith in God

When I seek to analyze my own faith in God — not my faith in Jesus Christ or the incarnation, which is something else again, but my belief in a world with God — I find myself coming up against what I would call the whisper of spirit; alongside it, as companion, is the sense of wonder, the sense that the reality that is myself and the world and the universe around me is not sufficient to give an adequate account of its existence.

The whisper of spirit itself and its companion, the sense of wonder that whispers to me too, are certainly whispers in the sense that they are spoken softly; they are not shouted from the housetops. For Elijah: "a sound of sheer silence" (1 Kings 19:12); for Jesus: the wind (same Greek word as spirit) that "blows where it chooses, and you hear the sound of it, but you do not know where it comes from or where it goes" (John 3:8). For all their subtlety and delicacy, the whispers have one immense advantage over almost anything else: they are mine, right here and right now — they are part of my experience. When I was young, "faith" was spoken of as belief based on the witness of someone who could be trusted. The whisper of spirit and the whisper that comes from the sense of wonder are based on my own experience. I prefer it that way. It is not that I do not trust others; I do. I trust the weight of the community tradition that I am heir to. I trust the Newer Testament's witness to the message of Jesus Christ. I trust Jesus' message concerning God the Father. But when it comes to the ultimate destiny of my own life, my own faith in God, I am happy to be able to base that on something in my own experience.

When I wonder in doubt about my faith in God, I am comforted by that base in my own experience. I wonder if I am giving in to the weakness of fear and superstition: What if there is nothing before and after? I wonder if I am seduced by the promise of fullness of life after death. I wonder if I am supported by the social affirmation of those around me. It is a comfort to come back to my own experience and be confronted with the "whispers." I can be attracted to the simplicity of belief in a world without God, but the "whispers" will not let me rest in that belief. It does not tally with my experience. I can be attracted by the thought of faith in a world without God, but then I have to account for the "whispers" in my experience.

These are whispers, not neon lights, not the unavoidable, the undeniable. They generate faith, not knowledge. What I like about them is that they generate a faith that is not threatened from outside. Did the walls of Jericho come tumbling down or not? Is it so important? More important is the question: What was and is the point of the story? Did Jesus really walk on water and calm storms? Does our faith depend on that? What was the point of the stories? Were the miracles at Lourdes, Fatima, Medjugorje, wherever, genuine? Who knows? What do the stories of them do for people's lives? My mother took my disabled brother to Lourdes and brought him home uncured; she said her miracle was in being able to care for him to the end of her life. It was not the miracle she sought; she would say it was the one she found. The absence of a cure did not affect her faith. The presence or absence of the miraculous does not affect my faith. The whisper is there and there is nothing miraculous about it.

Different people experience God in different ways and describe the experience differently. Immanuel Kant, one of the West's greatest philosophers, wrote in terms of the incalculable vastness of the universe and the true inward infinitude possessed by the invisible self. Today, some speak of the sense of the numinous, evanescent in the way that it is sometimes there and sometimes not. Between the eighteenth century and today, many argued that just as a watch needed a watchmaker, a universe as intricate as ours needed a Creator God. Today we might substitute "intelligent designer" for yesterday's watchmaker, but cosmology and evolution are separate issues — and "Intelligent Design" is not regarded as science by most scientists, while creation and evolution are regarded as compatible by most theologians. "Statistical causation" eliminates much of the need for such design; we may not know *when* or *how* a given event will happen, but we do know *that* it will happen. Others would say that belief in a world with God makes sense of ordinary life for them; it does not matter much what intellectuals think.

One may pooh-pooh Kant's heavens above and conscience within or the modern's sense of the numinous. However, they are the experiences of individuals that controlled the decisions of those individuals. They are not the witness of another; they are the experiences of the people themselves. Many would be aware that, given the possibility of a single chance against all odds, the watchmaker God is not an incontrovertible argument; chance is always a possibility. But if they had to place a bet, most know how they would risk their money — or, in the case of faith, their lives. What experience, betting odds, or sheer common sense have in common is the absence of dependence on anyone else.

Like the watchmaker idea, the "whisper" does not take us very far, yet from one point of view it may be as far as we should go. We reach the God who is "utterly other"; but, on these grounds alone, we do not reach the faith that includes God's incarnation. We can claim belief in an intelligent being that adequately accounts for itself. The claim from the whisper does not extend to the activity of God in the Older Testament or in Jesus Christ, although the Bible may evoke the whisper in its readers. Some speak of the whisper of the "utterly other" that they discern in the depths of their inner being. Whether this depends on some further aspect of faith we simply cannot know.

The God who is "utterly other" can be claimed as a being whose primary quality is infinitude. "Infinitude" as primary quality means that the adverb "infinitely" belongs in front of all the adjectives used of this God — infinitely good, infinitely wise, etc. It also means that we are infinitely incapable of saying more about this being we name God. With Ludwig Wittgenstein, great philosopher of language, we can say: whereof one cannot speak, thereof one must be silent (above). Augustine, great theologian of the West, said much the same, addressing the total mystery of God (trinitarian, therefore more than just the "utterly other" but nevertheless beyond words): to express *in some way* what we are *in no way* able

93

to express fully.[1] Chronologically somewhere between Augustine and Wittgenstein, Aquinas was no less blunt: "The ultimate in human knowledge about God knows it does not know God, insofar as it knows that what God is exceeds all that we can understand about him."[2]

Long ago, Augustine was well aware of the restlessness in him that could find rest only in the infinite of God. More recently, John Steinbeck had a character say the same in a rather different image: "There's a capacity for appetite . . . that a whole heaven and earth of cake can't satisfy."[3]

As a beginning, such faith may be minimal, but it depends solely on the believer and the believer's experience, uncertain though that may be. It is not dependent on anything or anyone else. Such faith is not dependent on the Bible, Older or Newer Testament; it is not dependent on the Gospels; it is not dependent on church doctrine. Such faith is not threatened by modern science or modern discoveries. It is grounded in the whispered experience of the believer in a world with God; it is a beginning.

Occasions and Moments

The whisper of spirit deep within those who recognize it is just that: a whisper. Its presence is evident to those who know it; its description is utterly elusive. Qohelet, "the Teacher," hints at it: "the eye is not satisfied with seeing, or the ear filled with hearing" (Eccl 1:8). St. Augustine wrote that "you have made us for yourself, O Lord, and we can find no rest until we rest in you." As a great mind, he was wise enough not to go beyond the general in describing how it was that what the Lord had made was restless. Elijah, the great prophet of the Older Testament, is portrayed going to Sinai/Horeb, the mountain of revelation, to encounter God (1 Kings 19). There was a great wind, splitting mountains and breaking rocks, and Elijah knew that God was not in the wind. After the

---

1. Augustine, *De Trinitate,* VII.iv.7.

2. Thomas Aquinas, *Quaestiones Disputae,* vol. 1, quaest. 7, art. 5, ad 14.

3. John Steinbeck, *East of Eden* (New York: Penguin [centennial edition], 2002; original ed., 1952), p. 157.

wind, there was an earthquake; Elijah knew that God was not in the earthquake either. After the earthquake, a fire; and God was not in the fire. Then next come three simple words in Hebrew — sound/voice, stillness, fine/thin — probably best rendered: the silent sound of stillness. Elijah recognized the presence of God. Wisely, neither Elijah nor the biblical author attempted further description.

If we too want to be wise, we will not attempt to describe the elusive. The whisper of spirit is recognizable to those who know it in many and very different circumstances. We have heard Jesus to Nicodemus: "The wind blows where it chooses, and you hear the sound of it, but you do not know where it comes from or where it goes" (John 3:8). Such is the whisper of the spirit, seldom found in the noise of splitting mountains and breaking rocks, of earthquake or fire; frequently found in silence or stillness. Mind you, Elijah is portrayed as a figure of solitude; small wonder he found God in silence and stillness. Had he gone to mass concerts or been part of a Welsh choir, his experience of God might have been portrayed in quite different ways.

The sense of wonder is little different. It can go hand in hand with the whisper of spirit; it can be independent of it. It can, of course, be associated with the realization of just how much we do not know about our selves, our world, and our universe. It hits rock bottom with the realization of what we cannot know: where reality has come from and where reality is going.

The whisper (of spirit or from wonder) may often be recognized; it can seldom be pinned down with precision. As noted, Augustine spoke of it in terms of restlessness; we seek a fulfillment we do not attain. Elijah recognized it in silence and stillness. Jesus spoke of what is momentarily present, its whence and whither unknown. We can hear the whisper — sense the spirit — deep within ourselves, in touch with a depth we recognize as belonging to our innermost selves. We can hear the whisper when we find ourselves in close harmony with our surroundings in ways that transcend ourselves. We can hear the whisper when we find ourselves taken beyond ourselves or outside ourselves, taken beyond the bodily limits of our being.

We can recognize the whisper in the longing for intimacy: the tenderness of touch, the commingling of selves; but the bonding of beings rather more than of bodies. Movement beyond the ordinary — skiing, surfing, skydiving, skateboarding, or whatever — reveals glimpses of the unlimited and underscores the longing within us to escape the limitedness of our physicality. Exaltation touches on the unlimited and evokes a rare aspect of our selves.

We do not control the whisper. We do not command it. We cannot summon its experience. When it is there, we may recognize it or realize that we have missed it. The "it" is our sense of the spirit, our sense of wonder before reality's insufficiency.

A listing of all the occasions that solicit such experience is impossible. It would also be tiresome. On the other hand, some examples may put flesh on the abstract skeleton we are talking about. Four headings will be enough: limitless silence; the unusual; the ordinary; limitless size.

Limitless Silence

Far away from the city lights, the sky overhead is totally dark, with a zillion pinpoints of light from the stars. We can lean back and look up or lie flat on our backs and gaze. Above us is an infinity of silent darkness. The air is cool and fresh. The wonder of it can evoke in us awareness of our longing beyond limit, of something within us that resonates with the limitless extent before us. We can echo the words of the psalm:

> When I look at your heavens, the work of your fingers,
>> the moon and the stars that you have established;
> what are human beings that you are mindful of them,
>> mortals that you care for them?
>
> (Ps 8:3-4 [Heb., 8:4-5])

We moderns may know about galaxies and the twinkle of starlight, the myriad stars in our own galaxy, the myriad galaxies in our universe, the possible extent of our universe beyond the limits our technology can observe, or the possibility of a multiverse with universes beyond our own. The wonder of it is not less great for us than for the ancients.

Our focus for the moment, here, is not the wonder of God's care for us humans but the whisper of spirit in us as we watch. For all the defined limits of our bodies, we are attracted to the limitless before us. It is not simply wonder at what we see; there can be an ache for what is beyond us. The whisper that comes from the sense of wonder may touch us too: all of this vastness that does not explain itself. Extraordinary fluke or extraordinary God? Uncaused universe or uncaused cause? We do not know; we hear the whisper; we wonder.

I do not know, but much the same may occur for us in a desert, under the searing sun, confronted by dune after dune of silent sand. The limitless before us speaks to the unlimited within us.

The yogi of Eastern religions has the experience of being in touch with the infinite, of being one with ultimate unity. For some, enlightenment is attained for periods of time; for others, it may be momentary. At such times, the whisper of spirit may perhaps be at hand.

In the silence and awe of a great building or a holy place, a whisper may be heard, a momentary flicker felt of something greater than ourselves.

The Unusual

Varieties of movement that go beyond our normal physical motion can bring home to us the limitedness of our normal functioning and touch the longing to go beyond it. The awareness of our ordinary limitedness can trigger our exultation at being released into the extraordinary.

There is the skier's exhilaration, slipping over the edge of a cornice and exulting in the challenge of a thousand-foot drop to the valley below, or the skier's elation at the top of a run, poised embracing the breathtaking vista of a seemingly limitless expanse of untouched snow and the prospect of a sweeping descent of effortless ease. There is the surfer's plunge down the face of a towering wave, aware of the awesome power within that wall of water momentarily mastered. There is the skateboarder's mastery of motion and supremacy over gravity. There is the hang-glider pilot, floating on air — aware of its fluidity and lift, its invisible ripples and eddies, its perilous intimacy. In the moment or in its memory, there can be that whisper of the spirit to be heard.

In unusual circumstances, we can be taken out of ourselves and put in touch with a sense of the absence of limit. It can happen when we are absorbed into a massed crowd — vastly larger than the individuals who make it up — at a rock concert or a football game, wherever we find ourselves caught up and taken out of ourselves. It can happen in the contemplation of art or in the listening to a symphony or a song. Something is evoked in us that we sense as more than material; it is often the whisper of spirit.

The Ordinary

Scattered across the ordinary humdrum course of daily life, there can be moments when we are suddenly aware of the numinous, when we can be touched by the whisper of spirit.

It can be in little things like intensity of focus on the unfolding of a flower or a simple beauty that is noticed. It can come with an unexpected moment of quiet in prayer, a quiet walk in the cool of evening, or a moment of silence between close friends (as the French say: "un ange qui passe," an angel that passes by). It may be triggered by the trickle of water in a little rivulet or the majestic flow of a great river, passing endlessly by, coming from and going to and never motionless before us.

It is hopeless to try and list such moments; these are pointers, no more. There are such moments; we know them when they happen. They are splendidly unpredictable and take us by surprise. The whisper of spirit is sometimes there.

Something else should not be overlooked: the comfort of the usual and the ordinary, in which the presence of spirit and wonder before the awareness of insufficiency are taken for granted. The whisper is sometimes there within that comfort.

Limitless Size

Other moments are more predictable. Above all, mountains and oceans can evoke for us the wonder of the vast, bringing out the echo of spirit in our beings.

Seen from below, at the right time, caught in the right light, mountains can appear as infinite masses of towering rock or huge shapes of shining snow. Seen from above, while resting briefly on a peak, mountains in fair weather offer a silent world of their own, stretching to horizons out of sight, motionless in gleaming snow until mist shrouds their distances. For the dwarfed observer, the whisper of spirit can be there.

Oceans too have a vast limitlessness all their own. Whether seen looking seaward from some beach or outward from some clifftop, the restlessness and the vastness can hold a human gaze. Beyond horizons near or far, we know great oceans go on and on. It is not just awe and wonder before the immensity of power, so restless, so irresistible; something is evoked in us by the immensity itself that is not ours but that touches the limitlessness that is somehow in us.

We could go on endlessly. Words point; they seldom capture. Those who have experienced this whisper of spirit know what is meant; those who have not do not. The experience may be explained, but not explained away; the experience cannot be dismissed.

Discussing conviction about theories in physics, Brian Greene remarks with insight: "Physicists also believe these theories are on the right track because, in some hard-to-describe way, they *feel* right. . . ."[4] Broadening this, we might say that those who believe in a world without God consider their belief to be on the right track because, in some hard-to-describe way, it *feels* right; belief in a God does not *feel* right. On the other hand, we might equally say that those who believe in a world with God consider their belief to be on the right track because, in some hard-to-describe way, it *feels* right; belief in a world without God does not *feel* right. Call it intuition, call it whisper, call it faith; it suffuses the condition in which we live.

Often associated with the sense of spirit is the awareness of wonder. "Wonder" is an abstract term that will do to name the sense in us that the immensity of what we experience does not adequately explain itself. In all cultures, myths have been woven to account for what is there. The myths may not mean much to us, especially if we are un-

---

4. Brian Greene, *The Fabric of the Cosmos: Space, Time, and the Texture of Reality* (New York: Knopf, 2004), p. 225.

schooled in their symbolism. All myths of origins, however, put in words a common conviction: what we experience needs to be accounted for. It is not a matter of unscientific people being ignorant of a scientific world. Those most aware of the mysteries of modern science are most aware of science's inability to go beyond the first beginnings to what may have been becoming. The insufficiency is there. Extraordinary fluke or extraordinary God; it is there. Uncaused universe or uncaused cause?

The mountain is there; the ocean is there; the flower is there; we are there. We question why. We do not know. There is a sense of wonder. For many, God is an answer. For others, God is no answer. We do not know; we have no better answer. We may wish to ignore it, but the sense of wonder is there. So is the whisper of spirit. Ignorance or insight? We choose.

Some say that their belief in a world with God is inspired by the awesomeness of nature. This "awesomeness of nature" holds together both something of the whisper of spirit and something of what we have been calling the sense of wonder. This same "awesomeness of nature" has echoes of the watchmaker argument. It cannot generate certainty for us; it may point to probability.

The whisper of spirit points to our longing for something *more,* something in ourselves beyond what we experience. The whisper that comes from our sense of wonder points to our awareness of need for something *other,* something beyond what we see that accounts for what we see. From different angles, both point in the direction of belief in a world with God. The whispers do not compel, they need not convince; they point. They are whispers.

The quintessential quality of whisper may lie in its very softness, its openness to being heard so differently. One of us may hear a whisper of spirit: here am I in a world with God — so here I am and what am I going to do about it? Another may hear a whisper of wonder: here am I in a world without God — so here I am and what am I going to do about it? A third may never be still enough to hear any whisper at all.

At the end of it all, the whisper of spirit evokes a need for meaning and, in a world with God, I find meaning in some areas of life; I despair of finding meaning in a world without God.

PART TWO

Belief in God's Love

CHAPTER 5

Belief in God's Love

Two questions matter most in life: Is there a God and is that God well-disposed toward us? We have been talking about the first; it is time to talk about the second.

It should be self-evident and obvious that these are the two questions that matter most; alas, it is all too easily obscured. A conservative archbishop, now a Roman cardinal, once shocked an experienced newspaper interviewer who had referred to the virgin birth as a major mystery of faith. No, said the archbishop; if basic mysteries were wanted, the central two were: (1) Does God exist? (2) How is God disposed toward us? Surprising to the interviewer, especially coming from an aggressively conservative source — the archbishop in question; on reflection, absolutely right. Two issues of belief to be kept separate and to be treated quite separately.

But first, the short-term and long-term pictures need a glance to put things in perspective. Short term, the picture is familiar. In too much of the world, the day-to-day is marked by uncertainty and survival at best. For readers of this book, there is more likely to be the daily routine of rising, eating, living and loving, children's schooling and education, jobs, housing, car loans, and family finances, with the longer-term concerns of retiring, ageing, and dying.

Our imaginations may visit the long-term perspective more rarely, probably because it is utterly unimaginable. Scientists calculate the age of the universe, now estimating something in the 13-15 billion-year range. Theologians affirm God as infinite; no beginning, no end. Scientists ponder the extent of the universe, how much matter may be there, how big the universe may be. Theologians affirm God is bigger, infinitely so. No wonder we speak of this God as "utterly other," quite beyond the realm of human imagining.

The short-term picture can be comforting and supportive — at least in comfortable circumstances. God is there, caring. God may not be fixing things or filling gaps; but God is there. There can be a sense of purpose, a sense of security. Not quite the poet's "God's in His heaven; all's right with the world,"[1] but somehow not too far from it. All is not right with the world, we know that; but, in comfortable circumstances, acting "as if" is a most acceptable delusion. The uncomfortable question: Where is a loving God in relation to a world in which all is not right? Faith can believe God loves us. Facts point to a world where all is not right. Theology, reconciling the two, must accept a God who sorrows and grieves over the suffering and is angered where the exercise of human freedom has brought about the human suffering. Anger, grief, and sorrow do not deny love. Experience may suggest that, for whatever reasons, divine omnipotence — or at least its exercise — may prove to be rather more of a delusion on our part than an activity of God.

Practically speaking, the long-term picture can be lost to view. We humans have emerged in a short space of time (thousands of years, not billions) in a small spot (our piddling little planet) in a vast universe. Why should God give a damn? We can be fascinated by the age of the universe. Our human lineage is a lot shorter, and our future may be even shorter still and quite different. Nuclear devastation apart, many ice ages apparently last a long time (some 90,000 years); often, the warm periods in between are shorter (some 10,000 years). Apparently global ice ages overrule the phenomenon of global warming. The presumed causes (solar/human) are potentially quite different; so are the time-scales. It is possible that our present warm period may end sooner and more suddenly than we would like. It is possible; as so often in such areas, time-related calculations are most uncertain. Nevertheless, if the ice-cap specialists are right, the end of what we might term "the warm" may happen far sooner than the end of the world. With most of Britain, Europe, China,

1. Robert Browning, "Pippa Passes."

and North America under a couple of miles of ice for a long, long time, what would humanity look like? Why should God give a damn?

Statistically, humankind might be hardly more than a hiccup in the universe's evolution. Would we be worth more than a divine shrug? Is faith in God's involvement with us, faith in God's having become one of us, the supreme example of deluded human self-importance? Maybe. Maybe not. About the remote past of human existence, we know relatively little. About the possibilities of human existence in the future, we know less. About the likelihood of relational beings elsewhere in the vastness of the universe, we know next to nothing. Our knowledge is restricted to our own species and the statistical pinprick that the human race may be on the reality of spacetime. Can God possibly love us? The possibility can hardly be denied. We can love each other; could it not be possible that God loves us? The possibility is there for religious faith to embrace.

Over the centuries, many Christians have believed in a judging God. The image is unquestionably there in the Newer Testament, with sheep and goats, narrow and broad paths. Possibly, it is one of the longest-surviving delusions of human self-importance. After all, it is coupled with the idea of a biblical Creator God who brought the human race into existence and who would reward the righteous and punish the wicked. As we look at it now, could the Creator God of all our universe bother with such a trifle? Love is one thing; judgment another — and the dividing line between righteous and wicked is far from clear. It may be unbelievable to claim that God should love us; it is surely less believable that God should have created us in order to judge us.

Few people today are comfortable with the idea of condemnation to hellfire for all eternity, where in Matthew's language "there will be weeping and gnashing of teeth" (Matt 22:13) or in Mark's "the worm never dies, and the fire is never quenched" (Mark 9:48). The realization is worrying that when human beings imagined God doing this sort of thing to the damned, at the same time human beings were busily engaged in doing much the same to "disturbers of the peace." It is frightening the degree to which theology mirrored the society of its day. Regrettably, we are probably no exception.

Consciously or not, two factors may influence recent reticence about hellfire. First, an awareness of the age and vastness of our universe. Could a God responsible for all that universe be bothered with stoking hellfire? Second, a shift in public feeling about punishments. In most places, people don't turn out in large numbers for such recreational events as a public execution. If we understand ourselves as above such primitive vengeance, surely God should be!

There are alternatives of course. In most modern hospitals, when medical hopes have been exhausted, life support can be turned off. Nothing grisly about that. Relatives grieve their loss, but in favorable circumstances they know that the right thing has been done. Should it be different for God? When after the end of a human life, if it is understood that hope for betterment has been exhausted, would it be unthinkable for a grieving God to turn off the tap? If a selective breeding program does not achieve the desired results, the program is terminated. If a human life does not achieve the desired result, would it not be proper and a kindness to terminate the attempt, to turn off the tap of life, to allow existence to cease? Believers, theist or atheist, might never know whether their belief was false or their lives too shallow. No gloating; just no more being.

If we believe in a loving God, the question to be asked is: On what grounds do we believe? There is biblical language to support the idea of God's love. From the Older Testament: "You are precious in my sight, and honored, and I love you" (Isa 43:4); from the Newer Testament: "God so loved the world that he gave his only Son" (John 3:16) or "As the Father has loved me, so I have loved you" (John 15:9). But that did not stop Mark and Matthew from speaking about unquenchable fire and weeping and gnashing of teeth. Are we capable of hearing God's words of love at the same time that we fear God's judgment and punishment?

There is abundant evidence that human beings have believed in a loving God. There is abundant evidence for human beliefs that have proved to be deluded. Can we do better than cling to others' belief?

Surely the most compelling reason for belief in the possibility of God's love for us is the reality of our love for each other. If we can see the lovable in each other, even fleetingly, dare we deny God that capacity? To echo the song from *Annie Get Your Gun:* "any good we can do, God can do better." There is no doubt that on occasion we are able to find the lovable in another. Dare we deny that ability to God?

Of course, a devil's advocate might say: "Love is needy; God is not." A good try, but can love be reduced to the satisfaction of needs? Sexual desire is important, powerful, and related to the satisfaction of need. But sexual desire is not to be confused with the fullness of love. Love meets many needs, but is the satisfaction of needs at the heart of love?

If love can be more than need, we may dare speak of God's love for us. Christian faith in the incarnation affirms that God values human life highly enough to have become one with us. "God so loved the world." For Christians, the ultimate argument in favor of God's commitment to humankind, of God's love for us, is that God should have become active in Jesus Christ — in traditional language, that God should have become human — that the son of God should have become the son of Mary. If as son of Mary, but not son of God (i.e., without the incarnation), Jesus believed in God's love for us, the invitation would certainly be there for us to share in Jesus' faith. With the incarnation, with Jesus as the son of God, our faith in God's love is not a sharing of Jesus' faith; instead, we have the directness of our own faith in Jesus' person, son of God. The basis for that Christian faith is ultimately the resurrection of Jesus. Of no other human is that claim made. "God raised him up" (Acts 2:24). "God so loved the world that he gave his only Son" (John 3:16). When we couple these two faith-claims, incarnation and resurrection point with limpid clarity in the direction of God's love for humankind. Utterly mind-blowing, but open to belief.

Just how utterly mind-blowing might be indicated by a theological article titled "Earth Chauvinism: A Cosmic Hubris in Believing That the Creator Was Incarnate on Our Own Bit of Interstellar Debris." "Chauvinism" and "cosmic hubris" can be replaced by sheer wonder and delight that the God who is creator of all our vast universe should be concerned with our own little bit of interstellar debris. I see no reason why the faith involved should be categorized as hubris; rather, it is the wonderful and humbling mystery of being loved, a wonder multiplied to the power of infinity. It is a huge act of faith; it is an incredible affirmation of human lovableness; it is a quiet acceptance that the God who is "utterly other" is utterly beyond the reach of even the haughtiest of human hubris.

The question returns: Did God intentionally create humankind or should we rather say that God was delighted and almost relieved when humankind came along in the evolutionary scheme of things? Given the minute margins for error in the theories some physicists advocate for the origin of the universe, etc., intentional creation has to be rated a possibility. Evolutionary achievement has to be rated a possibility too. With a God accepted as utterly other, possibilities exist far beyond our human imaginings.

In whatever case, faith in God confronts choice. Does God's love embrace all people, all the good sort of people, or just the best human beings? Put another way: Does God's love embrace all humans, most humans, or only a few humans? Can we know? How do we choose?

A God of a Few

The "best human beings" would have to belong in the category of perfect people. The label, "perfect people," is easily understood; the description to go on the label is almost impossible to write. How are "perfect people" to be described? The legendary comment is: "Perhaps I can't describe one, but I do know this: I don't want to live with one." In fact, the comment is supposed to be applicable to saints, and saints are not necessarily perfect people. Might examples help? From the Bible, David, Solomon, and Jehu — to take three kings of Israel — certainly would not qualify as perfect people. To take three prophets, I am not at all sure whether Isaiah would qualify; Jeremiah and Ezekiel certainly would not. Peter, James, and John? All three rank as saints, but as perfect people there are grave grounds for doubt. Whether from life or literature, we don't do much better from the past or the present. Lists could be compiled; agreement and unanimity would be unlikely.

If we have been lucky, we will have known people we regard as utterly lovable. If we have been lucky enough to know them well enough, we will probably be the first to admit that they were not utterly perfect. As a rule, those who know others most deeply and love them most intimately know their flaws and weaknesses best. In Second Esdras (as the book [approximately contemporary with the Gospel of Matthew] is called in the apocryphal or deutero-canonical section of the NRSV), the figure Ezra is told: "The Most High made this world for the sake of many, but the world to come for the sake of only a few. . . . Many have been created, but only a few shall be saved" (8:1, 3). In the hypothesis of "the perfect," the few may be fewer than expected. Media heroes such as Mahatma Gandhi, Dag Hammarskjöld, Nelson Mandela, and Mother Teresa are promising candidates. The lurking fear is, of course, that if we knew them better they might not seem so promising. We have already noted Lord Acton's remark that few great men are good men. The conclusion would be that we do not look for the good among the great (cf. Matt 11:7-11). A further conclusion might be drawn: that the perfect few are not as many as we may have thought.

The "utterly perfect" may not be easily identified. Is it unbelievable, however, that God should share life with only such few ("the saved")? Would it be unthinkable or unbelievable that God should act like any stud farmer or selective breeder and preserve the best while discarding the rest? If the option of hellfire is replaced with the simple termination of existence, is such a possibility unbelievable? I fear not.

It has been said that the core theology of a sect aims at explaining why everybody else is damned. In that "everybody else" lies the flaw at the heart of sectarian theology. To be credible, advocates of the "God of a few" had better not include themselves among the few. Such prudence apart, is a God of the few unbelievable? There is no irrefutable argument against the respectability of such a view.

A God of the Many

Far more widespread, in my judgment, is the view that almost all people will share life with God ("are saved"), with exclusion from their ranks being reserved for those judged utterly evil.

The problem here is the credibility gap. The huge hole in the credibility of this view of God and the future is that it is just so comfortable for almost everybody — everybody we approve of. Only the "nasties" are damned. It seems just a little too convenient to be true, a little too human to be likely. It is certainly possible.

A particular shift in judgment over the years has contributed to that possibility. These days, almost nothing seems absolutely certain, certain enough that one's eternal salvation could hang on it. There are evils that are universally condemned: child abuse, cold-blooded murder, rape, sadistic torture, defrauding the vulnerable — to name but a few. Equally though, in almost all such cases it is possible to argue for some form of diminished responsibility. It may not always be popular, but an awareness is abroad of the manifold influences, past and present, that play on any human action or decision. Once, this was not so evident. Authorities were viewed with greater deference; what they condemned was considered wrong and what they approved was considered right. A person's choice was clear; an action was right or wrong. Circumstances were seldom significant. For whatever reasons, that time has passed. Now, responsibility for what is accepted as clearly wrong is nevertheless a matter for discussion and assessment.

Such a shift in general consciousness affects to some degree how humans pass judgment on others' lives. Equally, it affects how God is thought to pass judgment on human lives. Is there so much more that God might know that is not known to human observers? To what extent might damnable behavior in human eyes become to some extent forgivable in the light of divine knowledge?

Rehabilitation is a relatively new concept in our evaluation of moral behavior. The verdicts of criminal courts are not to be confused with the judgment passed on the worth of a human life. Worth is not a matter of a moment. Where a thief's hand is cut off, a sex offender irreversibly neutered, a murderer imprisoned without possibility of parole, rehabilitation is not in view. A moment has determined the whole. When eternal salvation is at stake, rehabilitation has to be thought of. In law courts, when appropriate, prior criminal behavior and the issue of rehabilitation are taken into account; with God, would broader consideration of experience and moral behavior be outside the pale?

A theology that endorses a "God of the many" allows for the "utterly evil" among some at least, but accepts that many more than may be apparent to human eyes might find acceptance in God's eyes. A strong case against such a view is difficult to mount, especially when the "utterly evil" are simply removed from existence — the tap of life is turned off — rather than their being punished eternally.

A God of All

Belief in God's "unconditional love" affirms that God's love is extended to all people and implies that all will, in due course, share in life with God. Does this constitute an invitation to sin without the fear of punishment? Of course not; how absurd! Does being loved constitute an invitation to lowered standards of living?

On what grounds might such an argument be made? The conviction is widely enough expressed; the reasons for it are seldom spelled out. Among them would appear to be: the human experience that *present love can be based on more than present worth;* the human experience that *past history and the complexity of motivation are often unknown to us;* the human experience of *surprise at discovering goodness or neediness where least expected.* Couple these, or the like, with a sense of divine benevolence toward us humans and an awareness of God as "utterly other," of the *divine transcendence that extends so far beyond our feeble imaginings,* and the groundwork is present for belief in the possibility of God's unconditional love. For Christians, add to these the witness of Jesus' life and the core of Jesus' message.

Present love can be based on more than present worth. The primary example here, for me, comes from parents. I have heard often enough: "It is not just their own lives they've destroyed; it's others too. Drugs, addiction, various forms of degradation — you name it. They've done it themselves; they've dragged others into it. It's horrible. But, for all that, she's my daughter and I love her; he's my son and dammit I love him." If we can say such things, why not God? Hardened trial lawyers speak of the genuine love expressed by parents for their children who are hardened criminals. Should we believe God incapable of similar love?

Past history and the complexity of motivation are often unknown to us. The primary example here probably comes from psychiatrists. Much of the time, we may feel suspicious of media reports about specialists who use learned ideas and polysyllabic words to excuse actions we see as unacceptable. Bloody do-gooders (U.S.: bleeding hearts) who will not face the realities of life! We are also aware that sometimes such people are right. Should God not be way ahead of them?

Surprise at discovering goodness or neediness where least expected.

111

The experience is one most of us have had, and it is reputedly confirmed by recent specialists in marriage counseling. The word is that top marriage counselors peeling people's lives back to find out what made them tick encounter at rock bottom a basic goodness instead of the ultimate badness that an old-fashioned and misguided understanding of original sin had led them to expect. On a smaller scale, most of us know the experience of the belief that someone felt badly toward us and then the discovery that this was not the case at all. Similar cases of defective awareness among us are innumerable. Why should not God be gifted with insight far above the human?

Divine transcendence that extends so far beyond our feeble imaginings. We know that faith in God sets God up as better than we are. We may not know what to make of all that, but we may be disposed to hope that in some way God may be able to see the lovable in each of us — even if, perhaps especially if, we are not very good at seeing it ourselves.

Imagine a newspaper list of history's ten least lovable people. The exercise is illuminating: Who do we include? After Genghis Khan, Adolf Hitler, Josef Stalin, Mao Tse-tung, who else should we add? Did Eva Braun really find Hitler lovable? According to biographer Gita Serenyi, educated and highly sophisticated Albert Speer probably did, without there being anything homoerotic about it. John Toland, British historian and no friend of the Nazis, wrote of Hitler that had he died in 1937, he would undoubtedly have gone down in German history as one of its greatest figures. What did Mrs. Mao feel for Mao or Beria for Stalin? How much is there about people that we do not know? A dose of agnosticism in this regard does us no harm.

Ultimately, there is so much murkiness and uncertainty involved in assessing human behavior and exploring its association with human identity that there are grounds for believing that God might find the lovable in all — even if only in some sort of smallest degree. The issue is there for all of us: What moves human decision-making? What tilts people to vote one way or the other, conservative or liberal, republican or democrat? Conventional wisdom says we vote according to our pocketbooks. Overly simplistic, surely. Logical argument, economic conviction, national or international good? Hardly. Yes, all of these things, and then, yes, there is probably something else. The "something else" is deep down within us, not easily brought up from our depths, but it is there. So we vote; we can even be passionate about our politics. Can it be believed that God is passionate about us? The best argument for belief in the possibility of God's love for us is surely that we love one another. Any good we can do, God can do better. The all-important move from "God *can* love us" to "God *does* love us" is evidenced in faith by the incarnation and the resurrection of Jesus, son of God and son of Mary.

A further aspect cannot be neglected, despite full awareness of our human incapacity to come to terms with the infinitude of the God who is utterly other. It is the seriousness of this life and the eternity of life with God. In my understanding, we are obliged to take seriously the seriousness of life; for many, life is too painful not to be taken seriously — with nature sometimes too harsh, society sometimes too oppressive, and people sometimes too callous. From the Newer Testament, we know the wisdom of John's reticence in regard to the future life. "We are God's children now; what we will be has not yet been revealed" (1 John 3:2). What I have referred to elsewhere as "the comforting Roman doctrine of purgatory" leaves me uncomfortably suspicious. My proposed solution (retaining memory of our past frailty and simultaneously blessed in the knowledge of God's love for us) leaves most people plain uncomfortable. The refrain I have heard from people is: "We will be happy in heaven." Surely, knowing one is loved by God is ultimate happiness. Can human memory be eliminated without the loss of human identity? Healed, yes; but eliminated, hardly. Is any of us so perfect that memory does not harbor regret? For me, "the comforting Roman doctrine of purgatory" is rather like a car wash or a finishing school. In the first case, you go in dirty and come out clean; in the second, you go in a rough diamond and come out a polished gem. Alternative views that I am aware of are not more helpful. Given the reality of eternity, my question is about the seriousness of this present life.

Given the reality of love for the less-than-perfect (and that is most of us), I wonder whether for all eternity we do not know ourselves in full honesty and know ourselves fully loved by God. Is there any reason we should not know, as we believe God does, the failures and flaws and weaknesses that have become part of our makeup? Is there any reason that, knowing these, we should not know ourselves to be loved by God?

Is there any reason that, allowing for our lasting regret, the knowledge of being loved by God should not outweigh everything else — for all eternity?

At the core of faith in a world with God lies an inescapable tension: such believers are committed to belief in the reality of God, knowing that they might be wrong and committed to belief in the nature of God, knowing that they might be wrong. On the other hand, those who have faith in a world without God should also be aware that they might be wrong. No faith, theist or atheist, should ever be smug.

All three descriptions of the nature of God in relation to human-kind are possible (God of a few, God of the many, God of all). Which do we choose? At a certain level choose we must. Can we be sure our choice is correct? Of course not; that is part of the reality of living in the uncertainty of faith, any faith. Because in this life we cannot know, we are eminently free to believe what we may find most convincing.

We humans are part of it all, but we are not all of it. It is right to say that God loves better than we do. It is right, but it may be limited. Reality includes those we love, in the strict sense of the word. It includes the still-born, the prematurely dead, the mentally disabled or disadvantaged, the physically handicapped, and so many more. These we must leave to the mystery of God's love. Reality includes what we love in a more transferred sense, ranging from the animal world (our pets) to the world of art and music, and so much more. These too we had best leave to the mystery of God's love. Reality also requires the further question: to what extent is our focus on the human an act of ultimate self-centeredness? It is good to be aware of the limits of our thinking about God. A God who is "utterly other" is not bound by the limitedness of our thinking.

Intercessory Prayer

Belief in God's unconditional love and the practice of intercessory prayer do not necessarily fit together well. Love wants to do what it can for the beloved. Those who intercede want something done for them. The fit is not perfect when, by definition, the lover (in this case, God) knows what is wanted. One suggested solution is hardly helpful: God wants us to pray. "Beg for it" may be an unlikely foundation on which to build a lasting relationship. In an incautious moment, Morris West writes of a deeply holy man "who urged mercy upon the Unseen Father, through the merit of the incarnate Son."[2] Does a God who truly loves need such urging?

We may need to urge for our own sake. But do we believe an unconditionally loving God needs to be urged and importuned? Do we believe an unconditionally loving God waits for our prayers before moving to action on our behalf? I know friends who unquestionably believe in God's unconditional love for them and claim to get furiously angry with God for not providing them with the energy and stimulus they need in order to do what has to be done. That is understandable enough. They are not angry with God because God has not done for them what has to be done. They are angry at God because they feel the absence of energy and stimulus that they believe God could give them to enable them to do it for themselves. Good friends can provide us with the energy and stimulus to do what we have to do. Why not God? The anger is a response to the felt absence of energy and stimulus. It is a spontaneous response to the absence of energy; it need not be a denial of love. Our belief that God does not normally override human freedom need not stop us from getting angry at God; it is often easier than being angry with ourselves. Logic is one thing; feeling is another.

Sometimes people — above all in times of powerlessness or fear — beg God because it is an instinctive human reflex. Dogs bark because they are dogs. For us, such a reflex may be indicative of the fragility of humanity that has to live out of faith. It may also be a gauge of the intensity of faith in God's love.

Without appealing to extreme situations, intercessory prayer may function often as a good weather vane indicating where our inner conviction is regarding God's unconditional love. "Pray for me, I've got a hard week ahead" is a totally normal request to make of a good friend. "Of course I will, but keep in mind that God loves you even more than I do" is surely a theologically sound response. "Thanks, I appreciate that; I'd forgotten it — but pray for me all the same" is just as theologically

2. Morris West, *The Clowns of God* (New York: Morrow, 1981), p. 239.

sound. However, if "pray for me all the same" is equivalent to "move God to action on my behalf," God's unconditional love is being given second place. If "pray for me all the same" means "be thinking of me in the week ahead," it is surely a normal request to make of a friend, or of God.

An understanding of prayer can be built around the analogy of relationship. In a relationship of unconditional love, intercession may not be needed but other things are. With God, they are properly part of our prayer. Sometimes we need to sort things out for ourselves to reach clarity. Sometimes people need to be quiet together. Sometimes people need to share needs and longings — for peace, for justice, for whatever — even if the beloved can't be expected to "fix it." Sometimes the sharing, with our God or with one another, generates the support and the life to act. Often those who love need to express feelings even when they know about them. Sometimes those who love need to hang in there with each other and at the same time keep a distance; tricky, but it can be necessary — even with God. On the other hand, sometimes we feel distant when we don't want to — with one another and with God. Sometimes we need to connect, just to touch base.

Communication has a massively rich role to play in the relationship between those who love. Prayer has an immensely rich role to play in our relationship with God. Like all communication, it needs to be worked at.

The Perennial Transition

Stretching back into the remote mists of belief in God and reaching down to each one of us today is the transition in religious faith from the God of the whisper to the God committed to us. In Karl Rahner's words: "There is really only one question, whether this God wanted to be merely the eternally distant one, or whether beyond that he wanted to be the innermost center of our existence in free grace and in self-communication."[3]

3. Karl Rahner, *Foundations of Christian Faith: An Introduction to the Idea of Christianity* (New York: Crossroad, 1978), p. 12.

Two statements stand out for me.[4]

Tertullian (second–third century) reflects for me our emergence from an ancient culture:

> Christ called himself truth, not custom.
> (Dominus noster Christus veritatem se, non consuetudinem cognominavit.)

Ratzinger comments: "In my view this is one of the really great assertions of patristic theology."

Pascal (seventeenth century) reflects for me the move toward our modern culture:

> Fire. "God of Abraham, God of Isaac, God of Jacob," not "of the philosophers and scholars."

Friedrich Hölderlin (German poet, 1770-1843) prefaced his "Hyperion" with an aphorism from just before Pascal's time (described as the "epitaph on Loyola," founder of the Jesuits, deriving from a 1640 work) that touches a pride in me as a Jesuit: "To be too great ever to be encompassed even by the largest and yet to choose to be contained by the smallest — that is divine" (Non coerceri maximo, contineri tamen a minimo, divinum est). Ratzinger adds: "The same idea occurs in a large number of impressive late Jewish texts." That the God of all should stoop to us, be concerned with us, is surely the greatest challenge to religious belief.

Ratzinger catches today's mood and the huge transition in faith from the God of all to the God concerned with us.

> Most people today still admit in some form or other that there probably is some such thing as a "supreme being." But people find it an absurd idea that this being should concern himself

---

4. The bulk of what will be said here derives from Joseph Ratzinger's *Introduction to Christianity* (London: Search, 1969), pp. 97-104, where the full references may also be found.

with man [sic]; we have the feeling — for it happens again and again even to those who try to believe — that this sort of thing is the expression of a naïve anthropomorphism, of a primitive mode of thought comprehensible in a situation in which man still lived in a small world, in which the earth was the centre of all things and God had nothing else to do but look down on it.

Not so, says Ratzinger. We may think we know better, living in an age

when we know how infinitely different things are, how unimportant the earth is in the vast universe and consequently how unimportant that little speck of dust, man, is in comparison with the dimensions of the cosmos — in an age like this it seems an absurd idea that this supreme being should concern himself with man, his pitiful little world, his cares, his sins and his non-sins.

The trap in all this is that our enlightened modern thought is still thinking of God "in a very petty and only too human way." For all our modernity, we attribute to God "a consciousness like ours," with limits like ours. For Ratzinger, the spirit we recognize in the human heart is in the eyes of God — who as spirit bears up and encompasses the universe — greater than all the galaxies in that same universe.[5]

The Perennial Wonder

The more I ponder this move from a God as creator of all to a God as concerned for us, the more I am forced back to an experience I reported in *God First Loved Us*.

I was saying to a friend how I hoped that there might be relational beings peopling worlds across our universe. She asked why. I replied that it would make the creation of our universe in all its immensity more intelligible. It would dispel that sense of

5. Ratzinger, *Introduction*, pp. 101-2.

human egocentricity, with us existing all alone in the vastness of an infinitely expanding universe. She looked at me and said: "Tony Campbell, if you really believed in God's passionate love, you'd realize that God loves enough to create the entire universe just for you." In that expressive Irish phrase, I was gobsmacked. My head knew she was right. But I couldn't get my insides around it; I still can't. Such love is unbelievable; I believe it is right; I still hope there are millions of other peopled worlds in our universe.[6]

Is it too much to believe that the God who is utterly other should have thought "Let there be," and that in the fullness of time we are? For a God who is utterly other, it could be utterly effortless. Three reflections hover:

Unimaginable?	Yes, of course.
Impossible?	No, not really.
Unbelievable?	Almost, but not quite.

At the end of it all, of the options open to Christian faith, I find belief in an unconditionally loving God to be the most attractive, most reasonable, and least affected by human prejudice and self-interest. The cross explodes the categories of common sense or calculation.

Returning to Tertullian's assertion about Christ who called himself "truth, not custom," we recognize its relevance still today. We may indeed have moved from a scientifically ancient culture to a scientifically modern one. The move from custom to truth remains with us as a perennial transition, and it will concern us constantly in the final part of this book as we move to the exploration of the possibilities of a phoenix church — letting go of custom, hoping to hold on to truth. One might argue all sorts of subtle nuances involving truth and custom, truth and tradition. We will refrain, simply because our task is not so much to be true to Tertullian as to be true to ourselves.

---

6. Antony Campbell, *God First Loved Us: The Challenge of Accepting Unconditional Love* (New York: Paulist, 2000), pp. 44-45.

PART THREE

BELIEF AND GOD'S PHOENIX CHURCH

CHAPTER 6

Faith in God and a Phoenix Church

The whisper of spirit, coupled with a sense of wonder, opens the way to the possibility of faith in a God who is creator and sustainer, who is utterly other, of whom we can hardly speak. For Christians, faith in the concern and commitment expressed above all in the person of Jesus Christ — his incarnation, death, and resurrection — opens the way to the possibility of faith in a God who loves us human beings, tiny and insignificant though we are when measured against the vastness of space and time — and of whom to some degree we can therefore speak. Two different responses for Christians: one to the experience of whispers and wonder, and another to the experience of Jesus Christ; two responses that blend into a lived faith that is one.

A clarifier is helpful here. The experience of whispers and wonder is clearly direct and immediate; it is our own. For many, the experience of Jesus Christ could be seen as indirect and mediated by the faith of others, from gospel-writers to contemporaries. It need not be so. The experience of Jesus Christ, for many, can be as directly personal and immediately their own as the experience of whispers and wonder. The impact of Jesus Christ can be experienced in the here and now, as personal and my own. It is not necessarily a matter of a distant past; it can be the experience of the present moment. As such, the two — the experience of whispers and wonder and the experience of Jesus Christ — blend into a lived faith that is one.

The oneness of that faith, so often accepted but unreflected, gives life an acceptability and an inherent value and meaning that matter. If there is no God, we will never know. If we believe God does not love, we lose a depth of meaning in this life and beyond. The faith that God both is and loves can be a context for meaning and hope. How is that faith to be supported and nourished? A response can take us to the phoenix church.

There is the whisper of spirit and the whisper of love. Love may be suspect when shouted from the housetops; usually, love is whispered from the depths of our being. To echo the language of Isaiah:

> Love does not cry out or shout aloud,
> it does not raise its voice in the streets.
> Love does not break the crushed reed,
> nor quench the wavering flame.
>
> (cf. Isa 42:2-3)

The whisper of spirit leads to the God of being; the whisper of love leads to the God of belonging. Belonging is a dangerous word, but its richness is worth the risk. Belonging can be thought of in terms of ownership; we can own belongings. But that is not what the word should mean when we use it in the context of love. Says the Song of Songs: "My beloved is mine and I am his" (Song 2:16). They belong to each other; they are lovers.

Religious believers can say that they belong to God, they are in God's hands. It would be most unfortunate if this acceptance of God's love were distorted by echoes of ownership. We *belong* to those who love us; we are not *owned* by them. To say that I belong to God is also to say that I commit myself in love to God; it is usually accompanied, not always explicitly, by an act of faith that is almost incredible, the claim of God's love for me.

It is precisely the incredible quality of this faith that needs the support of a phoenix church. Spirituality can stop short at the God of being or spirituality can move beyond to the God of belonging. Above all, spirituality is the art of living and fostering the life of the spirit, which can so easily be swamped by the unavoidable busyness of much of our daily life. The whisper of the spirit says that there is more than this unavoidable busyness. We need the times and rhythms to stop and hear the whisper. The whisper of love says that we are loved. We long for it on the human level, to love and be truly loved; it is utter gift when it is given. To allow ourselves to believe that it is given on the unutterable level of our God is to risk the totality of our lives on the whisper deep in our being that moves to belief in our being loved by God. Such belief needs support. What future shape of a church can best offer that support?

Phoenix Church

The phoenix is a fabled bird of ancient mythology — not to be confused with the city in Arizona. It emerged as resplendent new life when the ashes of the fire grew cold. How it got there and what the fire was doing in the first place need not concern us. What matters: the phoenix emerged from the ashes and gave new life. It is a good image for much of the modern-day Christian church, heading for the ash heap of irrelevance and needing a massive injection of new life. Of course, the modern-day Christian church is different in different churches and different places. My own Roman church has made a number of decisions in recent years that point its bureaucratic structures directly toward the ash heap. Alas, others have not been performing significantly better. In some cultural areas, Christian churches are flourishing; the future will tell whether much the same patterns exist that in time may bring them to a similar ash heap.

It would be an act of supreme folly for people of my age — or anyone else of today for that matter — to dare tell the people of the future how their church should be structured. What people of today can do is explore their faith and ask what kinds of support their faith needs or can expect from their community. That is what this chapter is about. A non-Roman friend of mine remarked: "Nobody of us can tell the other churches or denominations what to do. Many of the things you discuss are in many churches happening, many are not, for various reasons." No one dare tell others how their church should be structured. At the same time, no one today should dare think about the phoenix church without thinking ecumenically. Artificial barriers are just that: artificial. My Roman roots are obvious. Roots are good beginnings; the stronger they become, the more flexible the stability they offer. Hopefully, what works for some of us in some situations will be of value to others in other situations.

It is not a question of scholarship's recovery of the past and a return to some of the practices of early Christianity; it is a question of seeing how the needs of faith now can be met in the world of a phoenix church. It is not a question of how it was once in the past of the people of God; it is a question of how it might best be in the future of the people of God. Theologically central is the question whether this involvement of God in human affairs is seen as once-for-all (in the life of Jesus Christ before the Ascension) or as ongoing (in the living presence of Jesus Christ after the Ascension as well). It is God's phoenix church, the work of God's Spirit in human affairs, witness to the ongoing presence of Jesus Christ in our contemporary world.

This little book has not been about the intricacies of order, belief, and practice within the various Christian churches. There are too many. It has been about two major questions of human life: Does God exist? Does God love us? — and how does all this fit in with wisdom today (above all, modern science and cosmology)? The task of this final chapter is to explore where that faith affects life and ask what kinds of support such a faith needs or can expect from communities. This chapter is not about the differences within the wide range of churches, important as that is; it is about support for the faith that is common across this range — that there is a God and that this God loves us.

As a Roman Catholic priest, naturally enough I will be thinking and writing out of a Roman Catholic context. At the same time, I look for language that is open to experience well beyond these boundaries; others will judge how effective that quest has been. What should be evident — but may need emphasizing — is that members of each community must move beyond what is here, with reflection on how their faith in God and God's love is best supported and fostered at this time.

In the area of religious faith, there is often a gap between what people say and how people live. A caricature is easy: do as I say (uncomfortably strict), not as I do (comfortably lax); however, such hypocrisy is not what I mean. The gap I am referring to is subtle, delicate, and most important. It may be that the words used to express faith are not quite right, but they are identified with the way of life; in a crunch situation, adherents will die for them. What people consider worth dying for is to be considered important. The articulation, however, may often be more accurately found in the living than in the words. The gap can be between the beliefs we live by and the words we use to describe them. It is like a "separation of spheres" (in this case, sphere of living and sphere of language); it can be a widespread phenomenon. A couple of examples may help make the point clear.

One example is the Roman Catholic doctrine of infallibility. The claim made by the defining words is minimal, if attention is paid to the definition — the small print. The language used either by authorities appealing to it or by others appalled by it can suggest the awe-inspiring: divine certainty at the drop of a papal hat. From one vantage point, the impact on the living of Catholics is negligible. As noted earlier, since its declaration in 1870, papal infallibility has been formally exercised only once, in 1950 in the definition of Mary's Assumption — a definition that Swiss psychologist C. G. Jung considered "the most important religious event since the Reformation," because it exalts the feminine amid the masculinity of Christian faith.[1] Over against its formal use, the aura of infallibility may have been extensively exploited; the cynical might comment that any actual exercise of infallibility might have threatened the aura. The smart saying used to be: "Use it *or* lose it"; regarding papal infallibility, today some might say: "Use it *and* lose it" — if you use it, you'll likely lose it, by nailing your colors to a fragile mast.

Another example is the Roman Catholic understanding of real presence associated with the eucharist. The language can be awesome; the living is not. One theologian is reported to have said: "If I believed what Catholics believe about real presence, I would never step outside the church building." The logical follow-up should lead to the puzzled observation: "but they do believe and they do step outside and get on with life." Language about the eucharist (whether in John 6 or some catechisms) can evoke blood-dripping cannibalism; the eucharist as lived and believed is a liturgical gathering, involving bread and wine — and meaningful remembering.

---

1. Carl Gustav Jung, *Answer to Job* (London: Routledge & Kegan Paul, 1954), p. 169.

Old-style devotions or new-fangled religious activities may in theory offer apocalyptic promises or raise unreal expectations; in life, they
may be hope-sustaining activities. Morals may formulate words of unattainable theory; in life, compassion may be appropriate to pastoral
practice. Faith-healing may bother the skeptical; in life, it may enhance
faith and bring about a different form of needed healing. The spheres
are separate; the separation is subtle. Proverbially, the proof of the pud-
ding is in the eating; so here, much of the proof of the words is in the living. From experience, we all know that in some people's lives certain aspects of belief constrict horribly; we also know that certain aspects of
belief can liberate wonderfully. The causes are elusive. In a short book
like this, readers have to be trusted to identify what makes the most
sense to them and creates the most value for them in their context.

In one of his novels, Morris West has a fictional C. G. Jung reflect: "I
do not see man's myths and fairy tales and diverse religions as a crutch.
I see them rather as sacraments of healing, as symbols by which man
expresses his perception of mystery and adjusts his psyche to its bur-
den."[2] It can be so; it is not always so.

Like anything else worthwhile in life, faith in God is to be supported
and fostered. We have talked of two aspects of religious faith: faith that
God exists; faith that God loves us. In the oneness of our lives, they tend
to mingle. At one level, faith that God exists is an interpretation of experience. It is comforting to know that we are not alone in such interpretation; it is particularly comforting that others of respected intelligence,
insight, and wisdom share this interpretation of experience and so believe in a world with God. Comfort and support come from both quantity and quality, how many and who. Faith that God loves us is also supported by the quantity and quality of fellow believers, even more by the
caliber of their living. Faith in God's love for us, however, may need
more active and individual support and fostering, which is where the
phoenix church comes in.

Faith in God's being is grounded in an interpretation of our experience. For Christians, faith in God's love is grounded in a faith in Jesus
Christ that goes far beyond the whispered experience. It too needs to be

2. Morris West, *The World Is Made of Glass* (New York: Morrow, 1983), p. 74.

supported and fostered. Its grounding we have discussed above; now it is time to concern ourselves with the structures and practices that can support and foster it. For many Christians, such faith may be principally grounded in faith in the incarnation and the eucharist. Its support and fostering will tend to be centered around the eucharist, expression of Christ's incarnation then and presence among us now.

There are stages in our lives and correspondingly in our faith. For most, the middle stage is faith lived day by day in a world with God. Within that world, an earlier stage is the beginnings of that faith, whether at birth or in adulthood; a later stage in the evolving of religious faith comes when it is time to accept the process of leaving life. What kinds of support does this faith of ours need in these various times?

Place of Faith in Day-to-Day Life

Christian faith is usually lived in some form of community; mostly, such communities take the form of a parish (or equivalent). In their various ways, parishes provide for bonding, worship, and often the service of others. Bonding gives support to Christian faith, worship gives expression to Christian faith, and service to others is a concrete outflow from that faith. Gatherings can range in size from a cathedral congregation numbered in thousands to a small local grouping numbered in tens or less.

Foremost in such community or parish life is the pattern of weekly worship. As a general rule, such Christian worship combines a liturgy of the word with a liturgy of the meal. In some communities, the liturgy of the word is the primary, even the sole, element. We need to reflect on how such weekly worship nourishes and fosters faith; the question then is, how is this best done?

Common to both liturgy of the word and liturgy of the meal is the coming together of the group of believers, their connectedness and bonding. Churchgoers are by and large like-minded people who, with all the usual limitations, value and respect one another and spend time regularly doing something that in general all of them approve of. The community's worship and associated activities are a regular structural event in people's lives, offer meaning and a sense of purpose, and play their role in the people's integration into the larger God-oriented community around them. At a basic level, the regular meeting provides affirmation of the worth of religious faith in God and, if positive, the experience nourishes and fosters that faith.

The impact of hearing the Scriptures read is likely to vary immensely. It would be unwise to try and construct categories that encompass the full variety of this immensity. Despite this, it may be helpful to consider three samples: (1) hearing the biblical word as from God; (2) the act of hearing the biblical word as in itself a religious experience; (3) listening to the biblical word as a reflection on life with God, originating in a distant past and given revered status. A key issue for many Christian communities is how to understand the nature of the Bible: Does it, as God's word, disclose God's knowledge and will, or alternatively does it, as word of God's people, invite to reflection on what is desirable? For many, experience of the biblical text leaves little choice: the Bible invites to reflection.

Hearing the biblical word as from God implies a certain religious submission, akin to the suspension of disbelief in a theater, and involves setting aside potential distractions coming from critical awareness. Much of what was discussed in Chapter 3 regarding the Bible would remain outside the realm of a hearer's consciousness. The word is attended to not as an object of critical study but as part of a relationship with God. In normal circumstances, people hear what they want to hear and what they do not want to hear they do not hear; in this, hearers of the word from God are usually no different. What is heard, in these circumstances, is normally supportive of religious faith.

Hearing the biblical word proclaimed, especially liturgically, can be a religious experience in itself, not to be treated as part of a communication. Elements of the hearing — words, phrases, images — may attract attention. What matters is not so much the message as the hearing of the word, the creation of a disposition within the hearers that lifts them into the presence of the God whose word they hear. For the moment at least, the spiritual takes precedence over the cerebral. Because what is happening does not, at base, affect cognitive knowledge, in the experience the hearer's treasured beliefs are affirmed by the hearing.

Listening to the biblical word as a reflection on life with God may sound radically different; on close inspection, it may not be so. The totality of the biblical text offers a smorgasbord of reflections on human experience. Coming from human sources does not exclude a variety of possibilities for divine influence. What is felt to be of value is accepted; what is not is left aside. Discernment evaluates the impulse to accept or to discard. Is it motivated by sound sense or accepted community tradition? Alternatively, is it motivated by prejudice or self-interest? Critical awareness is allowed full play; discernment is influenced by insight and wisdom; religious faith is nourished and supported.

Homilies or sermons follow the reading of the sacred text. Their avowed aim, in most traditions at least, is the celebration and affirmation of the faith with which the reading has been heard, unfolding from the Scripture an understanding of God and of life, affirming religious belief and exhorting to fuller life.

Joined with the liturgy of the word may be the liturgy of the meal. Among Christians, belief in the eucharist encompasses a wide range, from the purely symbolic to the physically real. This is a book about faith in God's existence and God's love; it is not an exploration of various Christian teachings. This chapter is concerned with the ways in which Christian faith can be supported and nourished. The eucharist plays a central role in this support and nourishment; yet, when we examine this central role, position on the range of eucharistic belief, from symbolic to real, is surprisingly unimportant.

An understanding of how the eucharist functions in the life of a Christian believer is important for the functioning of support structures. We cannot be exhaustive or comprehensive here. We can, perhaps, touch on the extremes in the range. At one end of the spectrum, the eucharist as symbol alone recalls the Last Supper and the readiness of Jesus Christ to go to his passion and death for the sake of humankind. That apparently simple verb "recall" covers a huge gamut of experience. "Recall" can be the equivalent of no more than "remember"; "recall" can go much further in the direction of "be transformed by." It is wise not to underestimate the power of symbol.

At the other end of the spectrum is the affirmation, going beyond symbol, of belief in "real presence," with transubstantiation as it were the gold standard — at least within a now-outmoded philosophical system. It sounds overwhelming; the reality of course is not. Some abandon the belief as medieval superstition, hardly a good reason in itself if the belief is held by moderns. As one learned old Jesuit said late one night: "Tony, I'd ditch our belief in the eucharist tomorrow if it wasn't that for me the only real argument against the belief is that it is just so darned hard to believe." My sentiments exactly. Paul and the evangelists (especially John) had the language of sign and symbol available to them. They did not use it. They have the LORD say, "This my body" and "This my blood" (no "is" in Aramaic); for me, as for many, whatever the LORD meant is good enough. Today particularly, given our increasing awareness of the complexity of matter in the universe, we would be most unwise to indulge prejudicial opinions.

How does the eucharist in this understanding function as a support for faith — not as a challenge to it? In a thoroughly ordinary way, recipients take the body and blood of their LORD into their being. In an equally ordinary, but mysterious way, recipients are taken into the life of their LORD. One dares wonder whether the fabled orgies of the ancient mystery cults were as ordinary. Taking God into one's being or being taken into the being of God sounds like pretty mysterious and unhelpful language. As one person said simply when questioned: "I feel strengthened"; theologically, we might say "nourished." Simple language but powerful symbolism.

What is fascinating about this is the remarkable similarity between the "pure symbol" and "real presence" in terms of their function in the support of faith. Both reinforce the association of the believer and their LORD. Whether symbolically or really, in either case the LORD is taken into the believer. The effect is ordinary, mysterious, and undeniably real. Faith is supported and affirmed. In either case, the believer is absorbed more deeply into the realm of the divine. The absorption is ordinary, mysterious — and somehow real.

Mystery apart, most worshiping communities or parishes have a series of activities, ranging widely from babysitting and fundraising to caring for the sick and aged, all activities that in their own way support and nourish faith in a world with God. The key concept is service; the key effect is bonding or belonging.

Bonding, the intensifying of belonging, is an obvious aspect of the support and nourishment of religious faith. Working together is a natural bonding process, whether working for the good of one's own organization or for the good of others. Working for others is a natural outflow from religious faith. It may not be exclusive to the religious-minded; it is, however, inherent in religious faith. The ultimate reason for care for the poor is simple: they need it. Why others should care is articulated pervasively throughout the Older Testament by the reminder that Israel was once in Egypt (cf. Exod 22:21; Deut: 24:22), and that compassion is of the nature of Israel's God (cf. Exod 22:26 [Heb.; NRSV, 22:27]; 34:6). The conviction is equally pervasive in the Newer Testament (cf. the motivation in Matt 25:31-46). Outside monotheistic faith, it is a matter of humanity; a human community that does not care for its sick, its poor, and its powerless is not worthy of the name community. Done in the name of God, such activity nourishes and supports faith in God.

Another area where bonding and belonging are crucial is the delicate move from family dependence to independent adulthood. In terms of church ministry, it comes under the heading of "Youth Ministry." It involves a sense of bonding with one another and with the community where belonging matters. Traditionally the role of younger ministers and priests, it is becoming increasingly a specialist activity. Naturally, growth toward maturity leads into partnership and marriage.

The realm of partnership and marriage is central to human life ("it is not good . . . to be alone" [cf. Gen 2:18]). A community group needs to support its members in these moves, in their living together, and in the raising of their children. Support in these circumstances is not directly support of religious faith, but it is support for life lived in the context of religious faith. Life lived more richly through the support of the community group enhances the faith affirmations of that group. Support for couples in their living becomes support for them in their religious faith.

The shape that partnerships take will be determined by cultures and societies, not by books like this and probably not by the regulations of institutional churches. How churches can support such living needs careful reflection. People of good will and personal experience may not be adequately informed beyond the boundaries of their experience. People with professional training in counseling and psychiatry may be unduly intimidating. A middle ground needs to be found; it may not be easily identified. Three stages are evident: preparation for living together; support in coping with the problems of living together; affirmation should it happen that lives need to part. Different skills are needed at these different stages. Not all needs can be met; despite that, they need to be identified and acknowledged — not ignored.

An aside. In Roman Catholic circles, at the Second Vatican Council in the 1960s, an essential and overdue move introduced into the discussion of marriage the value of the mutual love and support of partners for each other. It was put on an equal footing with the previously (in Roman teaching) sole and central value of having children. Unfortunately, if the implications were foreseen, they were not sufficiently anticipated. The result, in the eyes of many observers, has been a pastoral mess, often of appalling proportions. Two factors have played their role. One is the Roman rejection of anything approaching the language of divorce. The other is an exclusive focus on the capacity of the couple at the point of their formal commitment to each other, with a refusal to recognize the possibility of change during the course of married partnership, either singly (for an individual) or jointly (for the couple). People are not snap-frozen at a moment in time, immobilized in life. Contracts may be made in law and even these may be open to renegotiation; commitments are more appropriate to life and may be open to reevaluation. Movement or growth is inevitable, leading to a deepening or an erosion of the capacity for commitment. The future will need to sort out the pastoral mess that has resulted, probably distancing the celebration in faith from the situation in law. The healing of hurt can be hugely helped by trust that God walks with us in the midst of upheaval.

While this may seem a matter of primarily Roman Catholic concern, the impact of togetherness and dissolution on families and life is of concern to all communities of religious faith.

More ecumenically vexing is the practice of confession, the sacrament of penance. Difficulties with sacramentality can smother discussion. The practice, although limited even in the past, of soldiers confessing to each other on the eve of battle hints at a human need beyond sacramentality; modern experience, although limited, can confirm the need. Forgiveness comes from God; that is clear. It also comes from those who have been hurt. Some public symbolizing of that forgiveness can still be needed, giving large-scale community rituals their importance. Private confession can be plagued by superstition and convention; the brevity of confessions and the rudimentary clinical skills of most confessors have raised doubts about the practice as a whole. But precisely the brevity and non-professional status may give the practice a particular value, located in abbreviated stock-taking, assessing stages and moves in life, articulating them for oneself in the presence of another, with a guarantee of brevity and without the threatening potential for therapy or professional involvement. Whether there is a place for such stock-taking outside the sacramentality of Roman Catholicism is not easily known. Past debates point to a duality of value: the once-in-a-lifetime approach, favored at some points in the past, most suits sacramentality (akin to evangelical conversion); the pattern of greater frequency, favored in more recent history, may point to pastoral needs.

Place of Faith at the Beginning

People can be born into the life of religious faith and later choose to stay in it; later in life, for whatever reason, people can choose to enter into the life of religious faith. The difficulty of transmitting values from generation to generation is age-old. "Another generation grew up after them, who did not know the LORD or the work that he had done for Israel" (Judg 2:10). "Knowing the LORD" and the work God had done for Israel is not a matter of history, in Israel's case any more than in ours; it is the transmission of values, of religious experience.

Parents surely instruct their children religiously by their living more than by other teaching. Values that are lived are communicated by example; the task of turning them into words for teaching is not an easy one. When it comes to schooling, whether within the structure of a school curriculum or outside it, teachers are best equipped to cope; gratuitous advice will not be found on these pages. Adults form a different category; of their own choice, they are seeking association with a group that offers a meaning for their lives.

For both groups, young and adult, there is the need or desire to know what the church they are attracted to teaches about God and contributes to life. The existence of God is basic; for Christian faith, the individual existence of Jesus Christ as a historical human person is basic too. Within the experience of Jesus is the role of the Trinity; within the understanding of Jesus are the issues of birth, ministry, passion, death, and resurrection. Baptism matters as entry rite into the group. Eucharist matters as nourishment of the group. The implications of all of this for the daily life of the people in the group matter enormously.

The exploration and communication of this faith is an invitation and a challenge to the skill of teachers, for youth and adults alike. Formation in these skills is so highly desirable and often so hard to come by. Rites to solemnize these moments may be confirmation for the baptized young and baptism together with confirmation for the unbaptized adults. Appropriate solemnization will be worked out in each generation, in each culture.

Place of Faith at the End

One of the great sadnesses of life is the recognition of diminishing vitality and the realization of the imminence of death. It is a sadness that need not diminish religious faith. In normal circumstances, it has been preceded by one of the great joys of life: of falling in love, the discovery of personal belonging, the entry into intimate and long-term partnership. Balancing the joy of love, the imminence of death can bring both the sorrow of parting and the hope of reunion; it can also motivate fear, whether instinctively religious or, more secularly, the loss of all that has been familiar. Moves that place such fear in a more comfortable context may be moves that support and nourish religious faith. The basic human decency of a community that cares for its sick, dying, and grieving can be reinforced by awareness that such care is a support for the believing community's religious faith. It is an avowal of the long-term value to be found in each of us — valued in turn by our God.

The stages are clear: the sick need care, spiritual as well as medical; the dying need comfort; the bereaved and grieving need solace and support. The death of someone we deeply love sears our inner being and challenges whatever may be unreflected in our relationship with God. Different cultures will meet these needs in different ways; different levels of sophistication and training will be required. Communities of religious faith that neglect these basic human needs will be inevitably failing in the nourishment and support of belief in a world with God. Treatment of this nourishment and support can hardly be adequately offered here. It will have to be enough to insist that it be provided and provided as thoroughly as possible.

Organizational and Structural Support

When we look back over what has been said, it is obviously important to make an inventory of the roles that have been identified. Only then can issues of personnel and training be discussed properly. Beyond people, there are issues of physical plant, maintenance, staffing, and finances. These latter are concerns that are common to many small businesses and the equivalent; I have heard the overlap put at eighty percent. In such areas, common to so many organizations, the special expertise associated with religious faith is hardly needed, provided that the common skills are not exercised in ways that are detrimental to a community of religious faith.

The inventory, then, that needs to be made is of the roles necessary for the nourishment and support of faith within a community that believes in a world with God. At the same time, a caution has to be expressed emphatically. In a future church, needs will vary from culture to culture, region to region, and even from ceremony to ceremony. The people of a phoenix church will work out for themselves how best to organize and how best to celebrate. Talking about roles and listing them here serves only to highlight the timeworn practices of yesterday's church and liberate our imaginations for tomorrow's church. No suggestion can be determinative; some suggestions may be illuminating.

Roles

The list of roles is extensive: for the community, a leader in faith; for the eucharist, presiders and preachers (the problem caused by the lack of an appropriate term will be discussed below); youth ministers and educators in faith (for the young and for adults); marriage preparation, celebration, and follow-up; caregivers for the sick, the dying, and the grieving; organizers for liturgies and celebrations — welcoming and arranging, celebrating with music, song, and dance, preparing for reading, facilitating eucharistic distribution, and so many other support roles. Behind the scenes in all this are the staff needed to keep the community organized and moving (secretaries, managers, maintenance, and all that).

It is clear that no one person can perform all these roles, no matter how committed the person or truncated the roles. To paraphrase Jesus, the roles are many and the people to fill them are few (cf. Matt 9:37; Luke 10:2). The so-called "vocations crisis" that affects most churches in the Western world will in time shift from "crisis" to "context" and the idea of "vocation" will need to be expanded appropriately. The tendency is widespread among ecclesiastical bureaucrats to blame those who are not responding to the assumed call; it may be more appropriate to blame the Holy Spirit for not issuing such a call. It may well be that the Holy Spirit is calling people to roles in the service of faith that ecclesiastical bureaucrats are blocking with all their might. In Roman Catholic circles, many of liberal bent expect married clergy and women priests to remedy matters. With only fragmentary and anecdotal information at my disposal, I nevertheless fear that they have not been listening closely enough to the experience of others. In many churches where married clergy and ordained women are already in place, the people needed to fill the roles are still too few.

The Spirit may be calling for a move from a focus on elite ministerial or priestly figures to a wider involvement of the community of religious faith in the living of that faith. Institutional western Christianity has tended to look down on shamans, witch doctors, peddlers of the occult, and the like. With no lack of encouragement from the institutions, however, religious believers have tended to look up to those responsible for ministerial or priestly functions, attributing something of a special quality to them. We hear language such as "my minister" or "our priest" and sometimes an aura of the special can be heard. It may be little different from "our doctor" or "my counselor." It can reflect no more than respect for extensive training and committed studies. In many cases, respect and reverence may be healthy and proper; in other cases, the unhealthy is possible. With a wide range of roles to be filled and with a wide range of people involved in them, the community finds itself taking more substantial responsibility for its own faith life. The shortage of "specialists" may be a blessing in disguise.

As the community takes on increasing responsibility and its members fill more roles in the life of faith, increasing clarity is needed about the preparation — faith formation, education, and skills — required for various roles. Faith in God needs to be nourished; faith in Jesus Christ needs to be supported and handed on. How is this best done? What formation is needed?

Where roles with the potential for major impact on the faith of the community are concerned, at least three factors are likely to be involved. First, a divine call, normally experienced as personal desire, and therefore subject to multiple influences — not all of them necessarily beneficial. Second, a commission or approval from the coordinating center or appropriate equivalent. Third, and vitally important, a call from the community within which the role is to be exercised.

It would seem unwise, perhaps also unjust, to exclude any of the able who may be willing and welcome to contribute to the nourishment and support of a community's faith in God. Divine call, appropriate approval, and local invitation all play their part in assessing suitability. Categories such as gender, state (married, unmarried, divorced), sexual orientation, nature of commitment (short-term, long-term), age (young, middle-aged, old), work status (active, retired; full-time, part-time), health (disabled, invalid), and so on play their part in assessing suitability; they should not of themselves determine suitability.

When roles are spelled out, the factors listed earlier become critically important: divine call (i.e., evaluated personal desire), commission or approval from the coordinating center, a call from the local faith community to be served. Personal desire has to be evaluated in the light of all the conflicting influences that may affect it. Approval from any coordinating center involves scrutiny of prejudice, questions of training and formation in Scripture, tradition, and theology. Finally, a call from the local faith community is essential; imposition from without makes little sense. It should be obvious how enormous a role is played in all of this by culture, structures of society, levels of organization within society, and so on.

Training

From the point of view of theologically careful and methodologically appropriate reflection, what steps ought to be taken in preparing people for the various roles needed? The first and absolutely necessary step would be the accurate description of the task to be done, of the role to be undertaken. If it is taken for granted that, in a phoenix church, the roles and tasks for tomorrow may not be those of the past, then what may be needed tomorrow must today be described tentatively and with great delicacy. Such description has to look to the needs to be fulfilled, the benefits to be achieved, the drawbacks to be faced. In the ecclesial situation of Christian faith, historical continuity with the event of Jesus Christ is to be taken into account. Continuity does not exclude growth; change is inevitable in a healthy organism; destructive elements need eradication and constructive elements need encouragement.

Along different rhythms and in different regions, impelled by the choice of what is good rather than compelled by the force of circumstances, a phoenix church may choose on occasion to gather for liturgical celebration in relatively small groups. Different groups will require quite different roles of both preacher of the word and presider at the eucharist. When selecting presiders and preachers, three elements need to be taken into consideration: the description of the task or role; the performance of that task or role today; the appropriateness of continuity with past tradition. The term "preacher" is unfortunate; for some, it can have overtones of a man mounting a pulpit to harangue the throng below. Replacement terms are not easy to come by. Homily finds favor in some Roman Catholic circles, but not necessarily far beyond them. One dictionary includes among its options for "homily": "tedious moralizing discourse" *(Concise Oxford);* not all that attractive. If we use "preacher" here, we need to be aware that what is meant is one who presides at the liturgy of the word. It is perhaps best to speak of a presider at the liturgy of the word (presider-word) and a presider at the liturgy of the eucharist (presider-eucharist). As will emerge, it would be a great pity to blend the two roles in one individual. To avoid such confusion, we will retain "preacher" here, but aware that in some circumstances we need something better, and with the hope that from creative imagination, subconscious depth, or fresh experience something innovative may emerge, something better than options such as focus-person, homilist, listener, reflecter, responder, speaker . . .

Preacher

Important aspects of the preacher's role need to be highlighted: to focus on the significance of the readings that have just been heard; to focus on this significance within the context of the immediate liturgical ceremony; to bring this focus to the concerns of the group participating in the ceremony or of the local faith-community that the group is part of; to extend this focus to the wider social context, whether local, regional, national, or global. Bringing focus to a liturgical gathering is important. In many faith-communities, the roles here distributed between preacher on the one hand and presider on the other have often been seen as the basic responsibility of one person. Guest preachers may be common; they are frequently seen as filling out the responsibility of the presider. What is being suggested here is simply that the two roles need not be subsumed under a single responsibility. Furthermore, the preparation and studies needed for the two roles may be notably different.

In this context, the quality of being a "listener" is important and appropriate. It brings out the aspects of listening to the word that has been heard, listening to the past (of tradition etc.), listening to the present (the local community, in all its diversity; the larger community, regional, national, or world), listening to the people present, then reflecting on what has been heard. Not: telling how it is. Not: telling a story. But: sharing what is heard and what is thought. We may not want different names for the role; we may, on the other hand, need a practice different from the past. On occasion, with good reason, people may want to share as well as hear, to be heard from rather than always to hear. The preacher's role has always been to help with the hearing of the appointed word, making access to it easier, breaking it open as it were. With increasing education in many communities and the great diversity of experience within communities, it becomes important for people to be heard from, rather than for people always to hear from another, especially a single other. Above all, the preacher must be a communicator, able to connect with the people of the community. A good preacher (presider at the liturgy of the word) must be a listener before being a speaker.

Correlated with the idea of the listener, the role of preacher has a strong element of the person who responds. The quality of "responder" has values that complement the quality of the listener. The sermon needs to respond to the readings in particular and, more generally, to the liturgical context. The sermon needs to respond to the social context in which those who are listening find themselves at a particular point in time. The sermon needs to respond to the concerns of its audience.

Reflective people are treasured gems. The quality of reflection fits well with those of listener and responder in bringing light to the role of preacher (or presider at the liturgy of the word). Reflecter suggests someone who is in touch with the community and its local and wider concerns, someone who can draw on an understanding of Scripture and theology, literature and the arts. The reflective comes from deep within, illuminating what is without.

Presider

The need for leadership and focus in a eucharistic celebration will vary with the size and solemnity of the gathering. In any Christian community, the focus role at a eucharist is not simple to describe. We can helpfully begin by imagining the variety of possible eucharistic formats. These can range from the pomp and circumstance of Canterbury, Rome, or other major centers through to the little church in village or country or the gatherings of believers in even homelier circumstances.

The rhythm of liturgical life in many churches might change considerably if religious believers often gathered regularly in small groups to hear the word, immerse themselves in the eucharist, and nourish and support their faith. The greater intimacy and personal depth (even warmth and humor) drawn from such small-group worship, or the inner strength drawn from it, might valuably complement larger and more formal community celebrations. It is possible that less pressure might be put on buildings and other aspects of physical plant, with their use more appropriately focused. It is certain that the requirements in numbers, knowledge, and training for eucharistic presiders and for preachers would be changed very considerably.

Concretely, instead of their regular weekly service, people might gather in smallish groups to worship two or three times in a month; once or twice in the month they might choose to worship in the larger community gathering. What might have served as the parish church would serve for the larger gathering; smaller groups would settle for homes or appropriate locations. At times, specialist groups within the local community need to gather. At times, the entire local community needs to gather. At times, cathedrals (or equivalent) are probably needed for the people of cities or larger regional groupings to gather in worship. The ideal is to have widespread choice available; the ideal is not to impose a particular pattern on people. The existence of such widespread choice, however, has its implications for the nourishment and support of faith.

Different needs at different times, different likes and dislikes, and differing traditions might result in weekly gatherings of this kind varying in size from smaller groups (perhaps 10-20 or less) to larger groups (perhaps 400-500 or more); the smaller allows for more personal interaction, while the larger allows for identification with a bigger body of people and, at times, even for a degree of anonymity and a blending into the crowd. The functions to be supported may be much the same; the number of functionaries needed may vary. If, for example, three thousand of those attending eucharistic liturgies over a weekend opted for small groups of 10-20, then the number of presiders needed for them would range between 150 and 300 (not beyond the reach of many larger parishes). Some serious thinking is critical. The two core roles are those of preaching and presiding; ancillary to these are reading and the provision of music; issues of welcome, general organization, and the distribution of the eucharist are more mundane. Discussion is needed as to how such functions are best prepared for and filled.

An important aspect of understanding relates to the choice of the term presider or celebrant. As role descriptions, presider and celebrant are not interchangeable. A presider performs the focus role at a liturgy, eucharistic or not, in which the others present participate. A celebrant of a liturgy performs an action that the others present attend. The two are not the same. To illustrate what is meant, it is easy to take examples from the recent changes in Roman Catholic liturgy.

With a *presider,* the participation of those present means that they as the Christian community are participants in the performance of the liturgy, including its eucharistic core. It is appropriately symbolized today by the priest in presentable vestments, facing the congregation and leading them in their worship, in their own language, with the people as a whole responding. The presider need not be thought of as the one who alone is empowered to bring about the reality of the eucharist; such power is surely part of the shared dignity of the Christian assembly. With a *celebrant,* the attendance of those present means that they as the community are present to witness and be associated with an action performed by the celebrant. For Roman Catholics of my generation, it may be appropriately symbolized by the priest in unfashionable and rather unsightly vestments, with his back to the congregation going through the sixteenth-century Tridentine rite in Latin, with the responses made in Latin by altar boys. With presiders, the congregation takes part fully and its members are participants; with celebrants, the congregation does no more than attend, and its members are spectators.

The difference has major implications for the focus role and those able to fill it. If men and women, young and old, single and married, and so on, are already in the eucharistic congregation, why should the appropriately commissioned and respected presider not be able to be

144

drawn from any one of those in that congregation? The story Luke has Jesus tell about guests invited to a great dinner party ends up with an invitation that is emphatically comprehensive (Luke 14:15-24). Invitations to preside may be more selective than invitations to dinner (in the context of the Kingdom), but should they be less comprehensive? We looked at congregations a little earlier. Participants vary as to gender, state (married, unmarried, divorced), sexual orientation, nature of commitment (short-term, long-term), age (young, middle-aged, old), work status (active, retired; full-time, part-time), health (disabled, invalid), and so on. Appropriately selected and prepared presiders could be drawn from any of these.

As noted, the role of the presider at a eucharist will vary as the size and nature of the gathering varies. In all cases, the presider is hardly the special person with special powers and special words, whose presence enables the eucharist to occur. In eucharistic gatherings, it is the Christian assembly that celebrates its eucharist and gives it reality. "It has been pointed out by many theologians . . . that the integral subject of all liturgical action — and this includes the action of the Eucharist — in the early Church was the *ecclesia* itself ['the whole believing people present'], never the 'I' of the leader alone."[3] To build on an Anglican insight, the presider is less consecrator than orchestrator. This raises the question of diversity in the possible understandings of priestly ordination in the future. Whatever the nature of such ordination in a phoenix church, would it be desirable to envisage a commissioning for the role of presider at specific eucharistic liturgies — with an appropriately increased number of candidates and assuming appropriate preparation?

Should we move from theological reflection to the reality of gatherings that have been occurring, we encounter the realms of the legal and the actual. Technically, the legal involves both the licit and the valid; the actual belongs in the sphere of the real, beyond the legal. When we move aside from authority's assessment, we may turn to the realm of the real, of what is and what actually takes place. What may be considered illicit by church authorities may still be viewed as valid by them.

---

3. Edward Schillebeeckx, "The Christian Community and Its Office-Bearers," *Concilium* 133 (March 1980): 95-133, p. 108.

For example, in many cases, baptism in the home by a family member without compelling circumstances would, according to the law of the Roman church, be illicit but valid. In a similar way, what may be considered as both illicit and invalid by church authorities may nevertheless be regarded by others as real. The phoenix church will have some sorting out to do.

The move toward emphasis on the implications of speaking of a "presider" involves a substantial realigning of the notion of eucharistic priesthood. The direction seems right; the mutual interaction of participants in the process has already begun — joyfully. Aspects of cooperation and complementarity are important. Commissioning, of course, is vital. Adequate reflection and nuance is not possible in the space here. Dangers are potentially latent in the "celebrant" approach, above all the potential exaggerations of an "alter Christus" (other Christ) theology such as: no women need apply; they haven't the physiology to be other Christs. When "celebrant" theology is rejected, the absurd notion (voiced by a good and influential pastor!) of having a visiting priest consecrate the necessary thousands of hosts for a month's use is recognized for what it is — absurd. Similarly, the "parachutist" notion of priesthood (floating in from on high), where the essential eucharistic function of the priest is to pronounce the consecrating words, is clearly revealed as a fearful distortion. In all too many cultures, a "presider" approach may diminish priestly power and mystique, shifting the emphasis toward service. A hard thing, clearly; a bad thing, hardly!

The traditional adage, "lex orandi lex credendi" (the pattern of prayer [is] the pattern of belief), suggests a major shift occurring in Roman eucharistic understanding. The shift is from the priestly celebration at which the people attended toward a greater emphasis on the assembly's participation in worship at which the priest presides. Patterns in prayer may be articulating realities that theologians need to catch up with.

"Catching up" is an important role for theologians. Some churches, notably my Roman Catholic Church, need to take account of past obtuseness. Centuries ago, the structures of society shifted from a landed aristocracy (involving birth and privilege, providing defense and leadership, grounded in a predominantly agricultural and strictly stratified society) to a commercial aristocracy (theoretically less fixedly stratified by class, based on big cities and the Industrial Revolution). Churches and theologians that resisted lost. More recently, the shift from the glories of medieval faith toward the insights of the Enlightenment (particularly in the treatment of biblical text) was equally resisted by some churches and theologians; they lost. At present, the shift appears to be from an era of centralized ecclesial power to one of decentralized inculturation. If the theologians do not catch up, churches that maintain their resistance are likely to lose again.

Certain currents in society are irreversible. A few women have always played significant roles in history. This was true in OT or NT times; it has been true in the Roman church, for example, whether Catherine of Siena and Catherine the Great or Teresa of Avila and Teresa of Calcutta; it has been evident through the power of certain elegant ladies among the English aristocracy or the eminence of the women who presided over the salons of France and Austria; it can be found in the role of significant women in much Western society today. Leadership may be for leaders, whatever their gender. Equality for women — symbolized in education, independence, and respect — has in the past been the privilege of the few; today that equality is being claimed by the many as their legitimate right. This is a shift that has not happened before in Western culture; its potential significance is probably as yet undreamed of. The current is irreversible, and should be. There are other irreversible currents. Homosexuals are no longer confined to closets. The disabled are less discriminated against than before. And more. These currents inevitably and rightly affect the way that society believes and worships. The way society believes and worships will affect the choice of leaders in that worship.

Where preachers are concerned, the difference between addressing larger and smaller groups is clear enough. If readings are taken both from Scripture and other literature, there will be need for the preacher to be at ease in the interpretation of both and in motivating the life of religious faith. Such figures need not be specialist exegetes. As such exegetes know, their specialist expertise is not best exercised in the preaching field. The nourishment and support of faith in God can be derived from the interpretation of Scripture; at the same time, many preachers know the worth of other sources that nourish and support religious faith. There may be a value in encouraging those undertaking the role of preacher to specialize in the arts of interpretation and communication.

Where presiders are concerned, the difference between presiding over larger and smaller groups is of course equally clear. The gifts of bread and wine will need to be brought appropriately to a focal point, the prayers said and the preparations completed. As at many formal concelebrations today, parts of the eucharistic prayer might be shared by several; the elements that are common to all might be shared by all. The culminating act of the distribution of communion would be achieved in ways most appropriate to the size and nature of the gathering. A final prayer and blessing bring this aspect of the celebration to a close.

Preparation for Supporting Faith

We have looked at a number of the roles important to the support of a community of religious faith. As listed before: a community leader; preachers and presiders for the eucharist; educators in faith (for the young and for adults) and youth ministers; marriage preparation, celebration, and follow-up; caregivers for the sick, the dying, and the grieving; lifegivers for liturgies and celebrations — welcoming and organizing, celebrating with music and song and dance, reading, eucharistic distribution, and so many other support roles. Behind the scenes in all this are the staff needed to keep the community organized and moving (secretaries, managers, maintenance, and all that).

In certain areas, many communities will not have the possibility of people for all these roles and will have to cope with that reality. The training and support for many of such roles is not to be expected from seminaries and theological colleges; it is better provided elsewhere. Traditionally, preachers and presiders have found their training and formation in seminaries and theological colleges. Within many seminaries (or equivalent), the tendency has been to believe students are being prepared for the manifold roles they will encounter in their work. The shaping of courses of study has struggled to cope with this de-

148

mand. With the diversity and multiplication of roles, it may become increasingly desirable to encourage studies preparing people for ministry to be more focused on the particular roles the people are expected to fill — leaving other areas aside. The needed adjustments have been creeping along slowly, in terms of the courses teachers offer, the courses students take, and the courses institutions require. The time will come when the process of revision will need to be more intentional. The roles have not yet received the clarification that allows the studies to be tailored to them.

As people live longer and as learning skills are often highly developed, it can make sense for people to devote specific time in preparation for what may be no more than a short-term commitment. In such cases, the nature of that preparation needs careful planning. Where tighter focus is given to specific roles in ministry (for example, educators and youth ministers, marriage specialists, caregivers, etc.), more restricted and more specialized formation may be desirable.

In many seminaries and theological schools, reflected in their various degree programs, the emphasis given to philosophical awareness, biblical study, church history, systematic or philosophical theology, moral and other issues, as well as pastoral preparation is a long way from a focused formation for limited roles. The people of a phoenix church will need to look at these roles in a variety of cultures and contexts. Significant leaders will always be needed in faith communities and, as such, will need and want significant training. But many are the roles that do not demand the qualities and overall training of these leader figures. Among these many roles are those of preacher at a liturgy and of presider at the eucharist. Faith communities are discovering and will keep discovering the skills needed by educators, caregivers, youth ministers, organizers and the like. It may be valuable, for a moment, to raise questions about the sort of qualities and training needed for those who will be the phoenix church's preachers at liturgies and presiders at eucharists.

Preachers need faith, aptitude, and the fundamentals. Faith and aptitude are easy enough to identify and the need for them obvious enough. Communities will evaluate aptitude appropriately; someone in the role of preacher needs the ability to communicate with people, to connect with the people of the community, to reflect on and integrate their lives with their faith. Faith is probably more difficult to evaluate and will vary according to community needs. The fundamentals are by far the most difficult to decide on. Familiarity with Scripture will be wanted; being at home in the theology and tradition of their church will surely be equally in demand. An awareness of pastoral issues will be indispensable, while the specific sensitivities and skills of the pastoral practitioner are less likely to be essential.

Presiders need the charism of leadership and presence, with a different bundling of the fundamentals. Some acquaintance with Scripture and theology will obviously be welcome. Essential, however, is a sense of their community's tradition and its practice in liturgical assemblies. Devotion to ritual has to be balanced by the flexibility that senses where a congregation is and what needs to be done to respond appropriately and prayerfully.

Essential to both presiders at the liturgy of the word (preachers) and to presiders at the liturgy of the eucharist will be an intimate access to the day-to-day experience of people, awareness of the joys, pleasures, and pains of ordinary living, as well as the routine dullness and quiet desperation or worse that can often be there.

The diversification of ministerial function implied here will have major implications for the life of worshiping communities. Most communities will need a central leader figure, the equivalent of today's parish priest, pastor, or minister. The demands on such a person will be quite different from today's demands. The pressure of regularly preaching and presiding will be greatly diminished. The challenge of leadership will be shared with those to whom it comes most naturally. The various skills of management and maintenance can be put to the community's best advantage, while carers, educators, and liturgical organizers, and all those others who seek to serve the faith of the community can be welded into a team to further the life and faith of the community. The advantage of all this: the community is invited to take responsibility for its own life of faith in ways that previously have been almost unattainable.

A couple of areas need noting. First, local communities of faith will always need leaders; the same is true, of course, of the larger regional groupings of communities. In many cases today, local communities are led by pastors, the products of seminaries (complemented by on-the-job experience and training). It is surely axiomatic that the most effective leaders of a community are not to be found exclusively among such "seminary-trained" pastors. Often, yes; exclusively, of course not. Two questions emerge. First, how do you select such community leaders? Second, what level of learning do they need, what level of training and formation? The questions are critical, the answers important, and it would be folly for the dying generation to dream of even suggesting to the phoenix generation how they might go about it. Past practice has generally not repeated ministerial ordination; priesthood has been thought of as priesthood for life, whether or not actively exercised. New inductions go with new positions; the original ordination remains and repetition is not needed. It is worth pointing out that, with a change in understanding, such leadership positions need only be held for periods of limited tenure rather than for the equivalent of life. In most communities, that will cause no problem. The reality of limited terms is already well known. We might add: serendipity is where gifts coincide with passion.

Second, communities of religious faith will always value people deeply steeped in the traditions of the community. In the past few centuries, in many traditions, members of the ordained ministry have substantially filled this need. In some communities at some times, there have been people, men and women, who stood out in terms of knowledge or experience, wisdom or holiness, or just plain well-informed prudence. They did not need to hold office within their communities; they were usually available for consultation and discussion. The generations of the phoenix church will know how to assist in their training and learning, how to identify and perhaps support them, and above all how to access their talents.

Three Separate Issues

Finally, three areas need attention when we look at the life of a phoenix church, at least within Roman Catholic circles. They are the place of cel-

ibacy in spirituality, the place of communities of religious life in a phoenix church, and the place of sexuality in future Christian living. All three
probably deserve a book each. Here, a paragraph or so for each will have
to do.

Celibacy and Spirituality

Celibacy, at least in the Roman Catholic community, emerges out of a
checkered past; today's concerns should surely be with its present and
its future. Alas, as part of that past, we have to admit with sorrow that
"Religious chastity or celibacy has always been defined in opposition.
Celibacy is seen as against what is physical, against the world, against
the sensual, against sex and marriage."[4] Small wonder it is too often
undervalued. Dubious claims have sometimes been made, engen-
dered by high-flown piety and spirituality. Religious intuition is one
thing; its expression in theology and law is another. In the modern
West, celibacy is predominantly associated with priests and religious
in the Roman Catholic Church. In the past and present of Europe, however, its appeal is not restricted to these. Looking at our world more
widely, celibacy's reach and importance are considerable. It has a significant place in Asian spirituality. It has long been present in both
Buddhism and Hinduism, with the possibilities of permanent vocation or temporary stage.

Quite clearly, for some people (whether women or men) celibacy
has been a fruitful success. Equally clearly, for some other people, celibacy has been an unmitigated disaster. The variety of reasons that have
impeded unprejudiced research in the area mean that we have yet to
learn why for some celibacy is fruitful and lifegiving and for others con-
stricting and disastrous. Of itself, celibacy does not disallow intimacy
and love — far from it. Celibacy refrains from the full pleasures of geni-
tal sexuality. Much more than that, celibacy excludes the coupling in
which two people bond in the complementarity and support of love in

4. Janette Gray, *Neither Escaping nor Exploiting Sex: Women's Celibacy* (Homebush,
NSW: St. Paul's, 1995), p. 12.

life lived together, in the forming of a family, with the having and raising of children, and in due course the delighting in grandchildren.
Doing without all this can be felt by many as relinquishing hugely significant aspects of a person's life and generativity. The counterbalance
to this sense of loss may be found in other aspects of immensely significant life and generativity. Janette Gray again: "From the accounts that
religious women give of their lives, celibacy emerges as *something rich,
positive and confidently human* though one would not guess this from
writings on celibacy."[5]

The balance between the sense of diminishment and the sense of
enhancement will vary for different people at different times in their
lives. Probably there are about as many ways of experiencing celibacy as
there are celibates. Certainly, generativity can be understood in many
ways and experienced in as many. Properly understood, celibacy is one
of the ways that people can rightly choose for living their lives fully. We
need to become more aware of what the impact is on their living that
can lead some people freely to choose a celibate life. Is there an impact
on spirituality that might lead some people to want others to make that
choice? What is the intrinsic value of celibacy? Does the prospect of
short-term or long-term celibacy make sense or make a difference?
Does celibacy have a contribution to make to the nourishment and support of faith in a world with God?

Religious Life and a Phoenix Church

In some communities, notably among Roman Catholics, the phenomenon of "religious life" has flourished in various forms. Has it values for
the nourishment and support of religious faith in a phoenix church?
Commitment has usually been expressed by vows; the number is imma-
terial (in some older groups, one; in general, three [poverty, chastity,
obedience]; for professed Jesuits like me, nine [for better or worse]).
The commitment has been to a way of life where mutual support in the
living of religious faith has been balanced by a commensurate degree of

---

5. Gray, *Neither Escaping nor Exploiting Sex*, p. 16, emphasis added.

personal sacrifice — above all, in the areas of ownership, family, and self-determination. In the past, the rationale for this commitment was often articulated in terms of a choice between "counsels" and "commandments"; it is an articulation that has been found inadequate and wrong. Structures were aimed at supporting faith through the prayer of the members (contemplative life), supporting faith through the service of the community (active life), or more usually a combination of both. Central to the phenomenon of "religious life" is the staking (in principle at least) of the value of a person's life *exclusively* on their faith in God, in all its uncertainty. The values stemming from personal ownership, family, and life choices are set aside in favor of values articulated exclusively in terms of faith in God. There are, of course, intermediate stages in such commitment; discussion of them here would complicate matters unhelpfully. Whether in the phoenix church of the future there will be a place and need for this form of "religious life," time alone will tell.

Sexuality: Love and Recreation

In many cultures, social attitudes and legal enactments have meant that sexual fidelity in marriage is no longer a primary factor in determining rights to inheritance and property. Similarly, medical and other advances have meant that sexual intercourse is no longer necessarily associated with the likelihood of conception. These changes have occurred; they will not be reversed. As a result, in a variety of ways, sexual pleasure and sexual intercourse have been given a safe place in the realm of social recreation that previously was largely inaccessible. What society cannot know until generations have passed are the implications of such recreational sex for the sex that has its place in the bonding of lasting love. For the moment, it would seem right to say that both aspects of sexual activity exist. Whether both can coexist healthily is a matter for future experience to determine. For the support and nourishment of religious faith in a phoenix church, this issue of the understanding of sexual activity will be important in a number of areas. For the moment, more need not be said.

Finale

A concluding look back over these reflections around the possible structures of any future church, a phoenix church, reveals the massive nature of the diversity and disparity needed in various areas. It has not been given emphasis in the text; the emphasis is there in the reality for any observer to see. As a result, the need for regionalism is overwhelming — allowing for differences within countries as well as between countries and cultures. Anything less would be moribund and impossible. There will inevitably be tension between the unity of the center and the diversity of the regions in any church. The handling of this tension can be left to the folk of the future; we of the transitional generations can trust them.

> I am about to create new heavens and a new earth;
> The former things shall not be remembered or come to mind.
> But be glad and rejoice forever in what I am creating.
>
> (Isa 65:17-18)

Conclusion

The whisper of spirit — and its companion the sense of wonder — suggests that there may indeed be a God. Rather than the outcome of an extraordinary fluke, our existence may be the outcome of an extraordinary God. To make this claim is an act of faith; to make any other claim is equally an act of faith. Whether we like it or not, we humans live in faith.

Whether scientifically we favor an inflationary cosmology or a cyclic cosmology, string theory or loop quantum gravity, we are still at present unable to account for how the inflation or the cycle started. When perhaps our grandchildren's grandchildren have settled this issue and determined with precision the theory of our origins, the ultimate mystery will remain: What, if anything, preceded our origins?

Extraordinary fluke or extraordinary God? Uncaused universe or uncaused cause? Faith in a God is thoroughly reasonable. Far more challenging — far more inviting — is faith that such a God of such immensity has concern for a relationship with humankind. The more the vastness of the universe (its temperatures, its densities, its speeds, and its sheer expanse) is hypothesized, the more the "bigness" that must be acknowledged of any God claimed in faith to exist and have a role. Of course, much more so if a plurality of universes (a "multiverse") is postulated. Nothing new here; it has been known since theology began. God is "utterly other" — the theological term is "transcendent." It is an extraordinary move, however, to affirm this God's love for that physically tiny element in our universe that we call humankind — us.

But that too is not new; it has been a source of rapture since faith began.

In all of this, there is nothing new. Philosophers like Voltaire, movements like Deism, certain elements of religions like Islam reach out toward the God who is "utterly other," the God we reach under the aspect of "utterly other," the God of the whispers. Judaism can answer Psalm 8's question with the faith expressed in its Hebrew Scriptures. Christianity can answer Psalm 8's question with faith expressed in its Hebrew Scriptures (nomenclature explicitly excluding the deutero-canonical books) or Older Testament (nomenclature open to including the deutero-canonical books), and above all with faith expressed in Jesus Christ. So we reach out to the God who is "utterly us," an aspect of God we reach only through a particular aspect of faith. Where there is error, it is usually in attempting to affirm something of the "utterly other" whereof we had best be silent.

For Christians, faith affirming God's love for us is grounded primarily in the life, death, and resurrection of Jesus Christ. Support for the possibility of God's love for us is given by the thought that if we can love one another, God can surely do better and see and love the lovable in us. Affirmed as one and the same, there is the God who is "utterly other" (God Creator and sustainer — of whom we can scarcely speak) and the God who is "utterly us" (God incarnate, son of God and son of Mary — of whom surely we should scarcely be silent). Faith in each derives from a different set of experiences; the whisper of spirit in one case and faith in the incarnation primarily in the other. Christian faith affirms both as one God; the claim of universality allows for only one God. Does this leave out the Holy Spirit? God forbid that anyone should be so stupid. In the traditional language of Western Christianity, the Holy Spirit proceeds from the Father and the Son, participating therefore in the "utterly other" and the "utterly us" — and we give thanks and rejoice.

Modern science is mind-blowing in the cosmological claims it makes. Modern Christian faith is mind-blowing in the theological claims it accepts. We live in faith ineluctably embedded in mystery — the mystery of ourselves, our universe, our God.

Religious faith is one of the ways of living in the ordinariness of the day-to-day; it is one of the ways of living richly in the midst of mystery.

Conclusion

One of the goals of this book has been to point to ways in which such religious faith can be nourished and supported.

In the end, what can we say of such faith? It is a slender reed. It is a splendid vision.

Bibliography

Armstrong, Karen. *A History of God. From Abraham to the Present: The 4000-year Quest for God.* London: Heinemann (Mandarin Paperbacks), 1993.

Booker, Christopher. *The Seven Basic Plots: Why We Tell Stories.* London: Continuum, 2004.

Bryson, Bill. *A Short History of Nearly Everything.* New York: Random House, 2003.

Campbell, Antony F. *God First Loved Us: The Challenge of Accepting Unconditional Love.* New York: Paulist, 2000.

Dawkins, Richard. *A Devil's Chaplain: Reflections on Hope, Lies, Science, and Love.* Boston: Houghton Mifflin, 2003.

Denzinger, Henricus, and Adolfus Schönmetzer. *Enchiridion Symbolorum: Definitionum et Declarationum de Rebus Fidei et Morum.* 22nd ed.; Freiburg im Breisgau: Herder, 1963.

Frei, Hans W. *The Eclipse of Biblical Narrative: A Study in Eighteenth and Nineteenth Century Hermeneutics.* New Haven: Yale University Press, 1974.

Fuller, Steve. *Kuhn vs. Popper: The Struggle for the Soul of Science.* New York: Columbia University Press, 2004.

Galbraith, John Kenneth. *The Affluent Society.* Boston: Houghton Mifflin, 1958.

Gray, Janette. *Neither Escaping nor Exploiting Sex: Women's Celibacy.* Homebush, NSW: St. Paul's, 1995.

Greene, Brian. *The Elegant Universe: Superstrings, Hidden Dimensions, and the Quest for the Ultimate Theory.* New York: Norton, 1999 and 2003 (new preface).

————. *The Fabric of the Cosmos: Space, Time, and the Texture of Reality.* New York: Knopf, 2004.

Gribbin, John. *Schrödinger's Kittens and the Search for Reality.* Boston: Little, Brown, 1995.

Habel, Norman. *The Book of Job: A Commentary.* Old Testament Library. London: SCM, 1985.

Halpern, Paul. *The Great Beyond: Higher Dimensions, Parallel Universes, and the Extraordinary Search for a Theory of Everything.* Hoboken, NJ: Wiley, 2004.

Hawking, Stephen, and Roger Penrose. *The Nature of Space and Time.* Princeton, NJ: Princeton University Press, 1996.

Hick, John, ed. *The Myth of God Incarnate.* London: SCM, 1977.

Jung, Carl Gustav. *Answer to Job.* London: Routledge & Kegan Paul, 1954.

Käsemann, Ernst. *New Testament Questions of Today.* London: SCM, 1969.

Kirvan, John J., editor. *The Infallibility Debate.* New York: Paulist, 1971.

Küng, Hans. *Infallible? An Enquiry.* London: Collins, 1971.

————. *Does God Exist?* Garden City, NY: Doubleday, 1980.

Le Carré, John. *The Spy Who Came in from the Cold.* London: Gollancz, 1963.

Martel, Yann. *Life of Pi: A Novel.* Orlando, FL: Harcourt, 2001.

Miller, Ruth. *Saul Bellow: A Biography of the Imagination.* New York: St. Martin's, 1991.

Pelikan, Jaroslav, ed. *The World Treasury of Modern Religious Thought.* Boston: Little, Brown, 1990.

Penrose, Roger. *The Road to Reality: A Complete Guide to the Laws of the Universe.* New York: Knopf, 2005.

Rahner, Karl. *Foundations of Christian Faith: An Introduction to the Idea of Christianity.* New York: Crossroad, 1978.

Ratzinger, Joseph. *Introduction to Christianity.* London: Search, 1969.

Rees, Martin. *Our Cosmic Habitat.* Princeton, NJ: Princeton University Press, 2001.

Sagan, Carl. *Broca's Brain.* New York: Random House, 1974.

Schillebeeckx, Edward. "The Christian Community and Its Office-Bearers," *Concilium* 133 (March 1980): 95-133.

Sen, Amartya. *Development as Freedom.* New York: Anchor, 2000.

Smolin, Lee. *Three Roads to Quantum Gravity.* New York: Basic Books, 2001.

Stark, Rodney, and Roger Finke. *Acts of Faith: Explaining the Human Side of Religion.* Berkeley: University of California Press, 2000.

Steinbeck, John. *East of Eden.* New York: Penguin (centennial edition), 2002; original ed., 1952.

The New York Times. "Astronomers Find the Earliest Signs Yet of a Violent Baby Universe." nytimes.com. March 17, 2006.

Updike, John. *Toward the End of Time.* New York: Knopf, 1977.

Waugh, Evelyn. *Brideshead Revisited: The Sacred and Profane Memories of Captain Charles Ryder.* Boston: Little, Brown, 1945.

West, Morris. *The Clowns of God.* New York: Morrow, 1981.

———. *The World Is Made of Glass.* New York: Morrow, 1983.

Wittgenstein, Ludwig. *Tractatus Logico-Philosophicus.* London: Routledge & Kegan Paul, 1961. German original, 1921; first English translation, 1922.

Young, Frances. "A Cloud of Witnesses." Chapter 2 in *The Myth of God Incarnate,* edited by John Hick, pp. 13-47.

Index